FESTIVE FEASTS

FESTIVE FEASTS
COOKBOOK

Michelle Berriedale-Johnson

THE BRITISH MUSEUM PRESS

ILLUSTRATION ACKNOWLEDGEMENTS

Biblioteca Nationale Centrale, Firenze: 69
The British Library: 20, 25, 40, 48, 50, 57, 58, 61, 65, 82, 89, 94, 95, 97, 112, 117, 118
The Trustees of The British Museum: 8, 10, 12, 13, 15, 17, 18, 21, 29, 30, 35, 37, 43, 53, 54, 55, 62, 66, 68, 70, 71, 73, 74, 80, 83, 108, 109, 110, 114, 119, 123
Chen Yu (photograph): 107
The Cleveland Museum of Art: 106 (John L. Severance Fund)
Corporation of London Libraries and Guildhall Art Gallery: 117
Mary Evans Picture Library: 9, 19, 32, 42, 44, 100
Field Museum, Chicago: 79
JewishEncyclopedia.com: 99
Minneapolis Institute of Arts: 92 (Gift of Michael Engel in memory of Celia Engel)
Museum of London: 121
National Gallery, Washington, D.C.: 31 (Widener Collection), 45 (Paul Mellon Collection)
National Portrait Gallery, London: 81
Sint-Pieterskerk, Leuven (Photograph © Scala, Florence): 93
Staatsgalerie, Stuttgart: frontispiece, 85
Eva Wilson, *100 Years of Ornament* (British Museum Press): 26
The Parson Woodforde Society: 116

FRONTISPIECE *Still-Life with Oysters and Pastries* by Osias Beert, 1610 (detail).

Michelle Berriedale-Johnson has asserted the moral right to be identified as
the author of this work

First published in 2003 by The British Museum Press
A division of The British Museum Company Ltd
46 Bloomsbury Street, London WC1B 3QQ

A catalogue record for this book is available from the British Library

ISBN 0 7141 2787 6

Designed and typeset in Centaur by Behram Kapadia

Printed in China by C & C Offset Printing Co., Ltd.

CONTENTS

Aperitif — and thanks

Imagine being given six months in which to dine with ten exotic figures from history — from any period, with no rules or regulations and no expense spared. This is what I was offered by the British Museum Press, and I have taken full advantage of their offer. No matter that my hosts are now only to be found in the pages of history books and the lays of ancient poets. They proved no less alive and certainly no less fascinating than if they had been here in person. My family and friends were all too happy to taste and sample, sip and savour in their stead.

Because my canvas has been so broad, to stay within my six-month time limit I have needed to lean heavily on the expertise of friends, historians and fellow cookery writers — all of whom have been unstintingly generous in their support. On page 127 you will find a list of the books you might choose to read if you want to delve deeper into the history of any one character or period. In the meantime, I could not send this book to print without thanking those who have journeyed with me through time and around the world.

Anyone who is interested in the food of ancient Greece must turn to the works of Andrew Dalby. A classicist-turned-food-historian, he has written extensively and entertainingly about the food, and the cooks, of ancient Greece and ancient Rome. His *Siren Feasts* and *The Classical Cookbook*, which he wrote with Sally Grainger for the British Museum, are both a delight to read and without them, Odysseus' banquet would have been hard to create.

Recalling the tantalizing smell of fresh fish sputtering on open-air griddles along the riverbank in the Baghdad of her childhood, my good friend Khulood d'Ami was inspired to spend hours combing traditional Iraqi recipe books for me. She also devoted a most enjoyable weekend to instructing me on dishes for the Caliph's feast — without her, it would never have happened.

Anna del Conte could fill twenty volumes with her knowledge of the food of her native Italy, both ancient and modern. Another happy weekend was spent poring over her copy of Cristoforo di Messisbugo's *Libro Novo*, which she translated and from which I cooked. To Anna must go the credit, and my thanks, for acquainting me both with the true history of Lucrezia and her delicious food.

The discovery of Joyce Westrip's book on Mughal cooking, and Bamber Gascoigne's *The Great Moghuls*, made this one of the most enjoyable chapters in the book. I would love to have had time to dine not just with the first emperor, Babur, but with his grandson, Akbar, his great-grandson, Jahangir, and his great-great-grandson, Shah Jahan. Should you wish to do so, I would recommend both books.

As Andrew Dalby is to ancient Greece, so is the late Sophie Coe to the cuisines of Mesoamerica. Her scholarship and her love of food shine through every fascinating page, and she introduced me to the wonderful Franciscan monk to whom we owe our great knowledge of the food of the Aztec peoples. Her seminal book, *America's First Cuisines*, is not only informative but a great read.

Claudia Roden's knowledge of the foods of the Middle East and of Jewish food from all round the world is encyclopaedic, and no one should write about Jewish food without consulting her. I also found an excellent book by Oded Schwartz (*In Search of Plenty: A History of Jewish Food*) which filled every remaining gap in my knowledge. But my thanks must also go to my good friends Tsvi Yeshurin, who encouraged, guided and corrected me via cyberspace from Tel Aviv, and Ralph and Jenny Goodstone, who sampled, tasted and approved the results of my labours in London.

And finally, I am indebted to my old cooking friend Dick Mieli, whose enthusiasm for the *Song of Hiawatha* and researches in the vast reaches of the Athenaeum Library in Boston made Hiawatha's wedding feast happen. Dick also introduced me to Beverly Cox and Martin Jacob's excellent book on American Indian cooking, *Spirit of the Harvest*.

However, none of this would have come to pass without the inspiration of my commissioning editor at the British Museum Press, Nina Shandloff, or would have appeared looking as stunning as it does without the unstinting efforts of my project editor, Miranda Harrison, and designer, Behram Kapadia. Thank you to them all, and I just hope that you, the reader, have as much fun using the book as we all had creating it.

Michelle Berriedale-Johnson
London

1

The Return of Odysseus:
A Homeric Banquet

Gilded silver beaker with curved lotus-flower petals and bosses, *c.* 300–250 BC. Excavated at Ithaca, the home of Homer's Odysseus.

In the introduction to his 1946 translations of *The Iliad* and *The Odyssey*, E.V. Rieu calls Homer the world's best storyteller, and you only need to read the description of Odysseus' final return from the Trojan War to see what he meant. Homer is thought to have lived between the seventh and tenth centuries BC, but the Trojan War, to recapture Helen of Troy, took place several centuries earlier. In *The Odyssey* Homer recounts the adventures of all the Greek chieftains on their return from the war, but his main concern is with the adventures of Odysseus, King of Ithaca.

Eventually, having survived the one-eyed Cyclops, escaped from the goddess Circe who had turned his men into pigs, spoken with the blind prophet Tiresias across the River of the Dead, sailed between the rock monsters Scylla and Charybdis, and plugged his ears to the song of the Sirens, Odysseus reaches the shores of Ithaca, nineteen years after he set sail.

During his long absence his son Telemachus has grown to manhood, while his wife Penelope, convinced that Odysseus will return, is still holding off the horde of suitors who have moved into the palace in their attempts to persuade her to marry them, and who are liberally helping themselves to Odysseus' best food and wine.

Odysseus, in the guise of a beggar, first makes friends with his swineherd Eumaeus, who has remained faithful to his master's memory, and then reveals himself to his son Telemachus. Over the best banquet that Eumaeus can lay on, they plot to overthrow the suitors.

Odysseus returns to his wife in disguise, and finds would-be suitors feasting in his palace. Challenged to handle the great bow of Odysseus, he shoots at the suitors. From *The Book of Epic Heroes* by Amy Cruse, 1926.

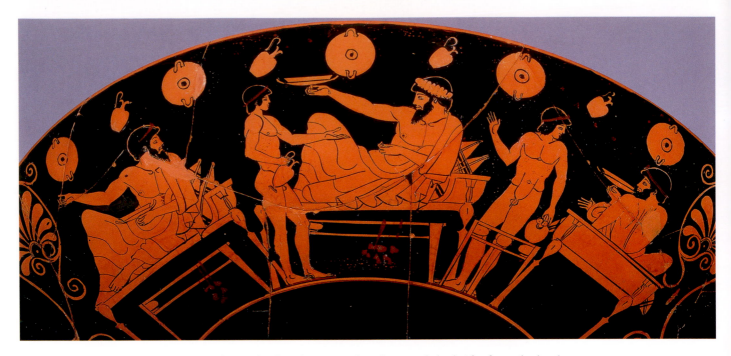

Drinking scene on a
Greek vase, *c.* 430 BC.
Cups and wine-jugs
hang on the wall.

The big sheep, the fatted goats and porkers, and the heifer from the herd.
These they roasted and served the inner parts and mixed themselves wine
in the bowls; the swineherd laid a cup for each man, the master herdsman
served them with bread in dainty baskets, and they fell on the good fare
spread before them...

Eumaeus then put before them platters of roast meat that had been left
over from their previous meal and with eager hospitality piled baskets high
with bread and mixed them some sweet wine in an ivy wood bowl.

Father and son plot together to overthrow the suitors besieging the faithful
Penelope. Odysseus enters the palace in his beggar's disguise, protected, as a guest,
by Telemachus and Penelope. A competition between the suitors to win Penelope's
hand by attempting to draw the great bow of Odysseus reveals that the 'beggar'
alone is able to string the bow. The hail of arrows which he unleashes kills the
most forward of the suitors. A pitched battle ensues during which the suitors,
though far greater in number, are all slain by Odysseus and his son. The reunion

between Odysseus and Penelope, who at first is fearful that the gods may be playing a trick on her, is touching and passionate.

The feasts throughout the story are frequent, but the menus rarely varied:

They quickly brought in the five year old bull, which they flayed and prepared by cutting up the carcass and deftly chopping it in small pieces. These they pierced with spits and carefully roasted and served in portions. And so they banqueted for the rest of the day till sunset.

And they prepared a banquet by slaughtering some full grown sheep and goats as well as several fatted hogs and a heifer from the herd.

Only once is an alternative dish mentioned, when the suitors taunt Odysseus in his beggar's disguise. They propose using 'the goats' paunches that we stuffed with fat and blood and set aside for supper' as a prize in a boxing match between Odysseus and a local beggar. Unattractive as these may sound, they no doubt contained barley or wheat and resembled a black pudding or even a Scottish haggis.

The fact that the only foods appearing in these banquets are roast meats, breads and sweet or sparkling wines should not be taken to suggest that this is what the normal Ithacan, even in Homeric times, would have eaten. Indeed, such profligacy with meat suggests major poetic licence, as meat would have been a rare treat for most Greeks. Daily fare included bread and cereal-based porridges (some sweetened with honey), milk and cheese from the goats and ewes roaming the hills, and fish from the all-encompassing 'wine-dark' sea. Although it is never mentioned in the context of a banquet, there are several references to fish in the last books of *The Odyssey*. For example, this is how Homer describes the slaughtered suitors after the great battle: 'They lay in heaps in the blood and dust, like fish that the fisher-man have dragged out of the grey surf in the meshes of their net ... gasping for the salt seas water till the bright sun ends their lives'.

Fresh fruits were also available to a nation of farmer-warriors. When Odysseus goes to his country farm to find his father Laertes, he proves that it is really him by describing the trees that his father had given him when he was young: 'I was only a little boy at the time, trotting after you through the orchard... You gave me thirteen pear, ten apple and forty fig trees, and at the same time you pointed out

Men collecting olives.
Athenian wine jar,
c. 520 BC.

the fifty rows of vines that were to be mine'. Herbs are not mentioned in *The Odyssey*, but mint, thyme, parsley, oregano, coriander, rosemary, fennel, garlic and chives all grow wild in the Mediterranean and would have been available to flavour the meat, fish and porridge dishes of everyday fare as well as the grander banquets.

'Flaying and cutting up a five year old bull before carefully spit roasting it' does not seem too practical a proposition in the twenty-first century. However, I have given directions for spit-roasting a whole lamb or suckling pig should the opportunity arise, as well as an option for roasting a more manageable shoulder or leg of lamb, kid, or pork. I have also given a very simple recipe for cooking black pudding, which is really tasty and sounds far more appealing than the goat's paunch stuffed with blood and fat! For those who feel that Homer should have included fish in his banquets, I have included a simple grilled tuna dish, as tuna would have abounded off the shores of Ithaca.

The 'baskets of dainty bread' which were served with those Homeric roasts are more difficult to recreate. Homer's wheat would probably have been *emmer*, an early wheat grain much like modern day spelt. Odysseus watches one of the

Women filling water jugs. Athenian cup, *c.* 400 BC.

maid-servants at his palace 'grinding the barley and wheat into meal for the household bread'. It is likely that the best breads would have been leavened, probably using the remains of the dough from an earlier bake, while flat breads would have been used for daily fare. I suggest using modern wholemeal pitta breads.

If you wish to be true to the Homeric menu, you should eschew serving any vegetables or salads. However, if you feel that you cannot face so much protein without any greens at all, a light green salad dressed with lemon juice, salt and olive oil with any of the dishes would be fine. To round off the meal I suggest some dried figs, simmered with some of Alcinous' pomegranates and pears.

Homer always accompanies his feast with wines, both flat and sparkling. This is often referred to as 'honeyed' or 'sweet' wine – 'black in colour, fragrant, and becoming fuller with age'. Indeed, Odysseus was presented with twelve amphoras of 'sweet unmixed wine, a divine drink' by the priest Maron in the course of his travels. As with all wines, this was to be mixed quite generously with water (up to twenty parts for some wines). A powerful modern Greek red wine, such as Nemea, would suit a Homeric feast, followed by a dessert wine such as the sweet and aromatic Muscat of Lemnos. Both of these can be found in most Greek delicatessens.

Spit-roasted Lamb, Kid or Suckling Pig

If you are roasting a whole animal you will either need an extremely large oven or to move the operation out of doors. The whole animal must be thoroughly cleaned and then well rubbed with salt and lemon juice, both inside and out. If you are using lamb, the stomach opening should be tightly sewn up. Whatever the animal, it should be securely attached to a spit.

The roasting should be started at some distance from the fire to prevent scorching, and then gradually brought closer to the flame. The cooking should take around 3 hours and the meat should be constantly turned and basted with its own drippings mixed with butter, thyme and lemon juice. A piglet needs roughly the same treatment although the cooking time may be up to 4 hours. Judging the right distance from the fire to ensure that all parts of the animal are cooked, without drying out the less fleshy parts, requires skill and experience. If you wish to do the job properly you should pull the meat apart with your fingers and serve it with fresh bread, salt and plenty of wine — watered or not, as you feel inclined!

Drawing of a plate depicting a battle during the Trojan War.

Roast Leg of Lamb or Pork

SERVES 8–10

This is a very simple way to roast the meat, and it allows the fresh flavours of the herbs and garlic to be fully appreciated. Serve in thick slices with fresh bread.

1 very large or 2 small legs of lamb, or 1 large leg of pork
8–10 cloves garlic — peeled but left whole unless they are very big, in which case halved
2 lemons
2–3 tablespoons olive oil
sea salt
1 teaspoon fresh thyme leaves
1 large sprig fresh rosemary

Heat the oven to 180 C / 350 F / Gas Mark 4. Cut deep slits in the meat and insert the garlic cloves. Slice 1 lemon and place the slices on a rack in a roasting tin, along with the sprig of rosemary. Lay the meat over the top. Mix the oil with the juice of the remaining lemon and the thyme, and rub it thoroughly all over the meat, allowing any extra to fall into the roasting tin.

Bake for 40 minutes to the kilo (20 minutes to the pound) for the lamb, 60 minutes to the kilo (30 minutes to the pound) for the pork, basting the joints regularly with the juices in the bottom of the pan.

Serve in thick slices, along with fresh bread to sop up any extra juices.

Goats Paunch

SERVES 10

500 g / 1¼ lb black sausage
450 ml / 15 floz / 2 cups water
2 teaspoons dried thyme

Heat the water with the thyme in a saucepan. Remove any plastic or other skin from the black pudding and cut it into 20 thickish slices. Add the pudding to the water and thyme, heat to boiling point, and simmer gently for 15 minutes.

Serve with a little of the juices in which they were cooked.

Griddled Tuna

SERVES 10

A barbecue would come closest to re-creating the conditions of the open fires of Ithaca, but a ribbed griddle or even a frying pan will also produce a good result. The tuna steaks are delicious if cooked only very briefly so that the centre remains nearly raw, but if you prefer your tuna well done, simply cook it for a bit longer on both sides.

Sea perch, bass and prawns are depicted on this fish plate from southern Italy. 4th century BC.

5–6 tablespoons olive oil
coarsely ground sea salt
leaves from around 20 sprigs of fresh thyme
4 lemons
10 fresh tuna steaks

Mix the oil, salt and thyme leaves with the juice from 1 or 2 of the lemons, depending on how large they are. Rub this mixture well into both sides of the steaks and leave aside, covered, for an hour.

Heat the barbecue, griddle or frying pan to very hot. Very briefly cook the steaks on both sides so that they are no more than seared. Otherwise, cook for 2–3 minutes on each side, depending on the thickness.

Serve at once with fresh bread and extra lemon wedges.

Fig and Pomegranate Sweetmeat

SERVES 10

This absolutely delicious sweetmeat ends up as a slightly sticky jam which can be eaten with a spoon from small dishes. Although there is no Homeric evidence for cooking the fruits in this way, these little dishes of conserve are one of the most traditional desserts throughout the Middle East, so I felt that it would not be too out of place at your Homeric banquet.

8 dried figs, stem removed and chopped into small pieces
2 fresh pears, cored and peeled and cut into small dice
6 tablespoons fresh pomegranate seeds with their juice
1 large wine glass of sweet white dessert wine
1 large wine glass of water
3 tablespoons honey

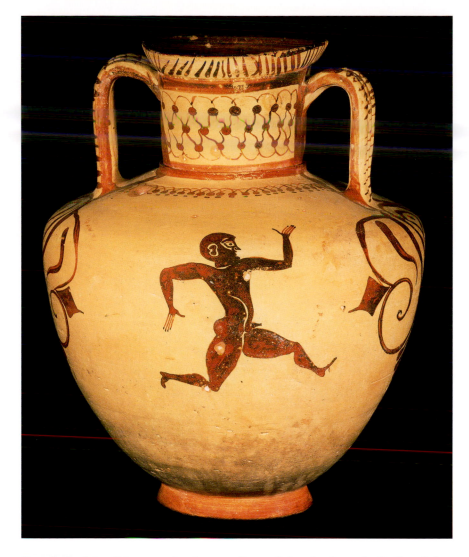

Amphora, with painting of a running man. Made in Miletos, Asia Minor (modern Turkey), 6th century BC.

Put all the ingredients together in a small pan. Bring slowly to the boil and then simmer, uncovered, for 45 minutes or until the liquid has all but dried up. Stir the mixture fairly frequently to make sure that it has not dried up or burnt.

Allow to cool slightly in the pan, then transfer to a decorative glass, ceramic or silver dish. At the end of the meal, give each guest a small spoon to serve themselves a little pile of conserve on a plate.

2

The 1001 Arabian Nights: Feasting with the Caliph

Gold dinar of Harun al' Rashid, who ruled from AD 786 to 809 as Abbasid caliph of Baghdad. A fabled patron of the arts and literature, he is cited as the ideal ruler in *The Arabian Nights*.

Of all the stories ever told, the magical tales of *The Arabian Nights: Tales From a Thousand and One Nights* must be among the best-known. From Chaucer's times onwards the enchanted horse, Aladdin, Ali-Baba, Sinbad the Sailor and the Genie have inspired writers, playwrights, poets and film-makers, and have been the stuff of every child's bedtime stories.

The earliest tales came from India and Persia in the eighth century AD. In the ninth century a group of stories from Baghdad was added, featuring Caliph Harun al' Rashid. In the thirteenth century came further Egyptian and Syrian tales. The final stories may have been written by eighteenth-century French scholar Galland, who translated – and expurgated – all twelve volumes and published them in 1717. Translated into English, this version captivated writers such as Daniel Defoe, Charles Dickens and Robert Louis Stevenson. The tales use a literary device known as 'framing' – telling a story within a story. The outmost frame is the story of Scheherazade and the supreme ruler, Shahryar. On discovering that his wife has been unfaithful, Shahryar decides to marry a new wife each day and kill her the following morning. When the supply of willing ladies runs short Scheherazade, the grand vizier's daughter, offers herself in marriage. On their wedding night Scheherazade's sister comes into their bedroom and asks her to tell them a story. The king is fascinated by Scheherazade's tale but dawn comes before it is done, so he postpones her execution until the following dawn when she has finished the story. The next night Scheherazade finishes the tale, but starts on another, and another . . . and so the nights go on, through all 1001 tales.

Illustration by Monro S. Orr of the favourite means of transport in *The Arabian Nights*.
Published in *The World's Fairy Book*, 1930.

Agib Entertained by the Ladies by H.J. Ford. Published in *The Arabian Nights Entertainments*, 1898.

The second frame, used in the stories from Baghdad, is that of the Caliph Harun al' Rashid. Harun and his foster brother Ja'far bin Yahya disguise themselves as ordinary citizens and wander the streets of Baghdad. The caliph gets to understand the troubles of his people, and each night they discover a new wonder or are told a new tale. Whether the real Harun al' Rashid actually wandered the streets of Baghdad is questionable. He was the fifth caliph in the Caliphate of the Abbasids, who had become absolute rulers of Islam in 750 AD. The Abbasids claimed direct descent from Muhammad, but in the 130 years since the prophet's death the caliphs had moved far from the days when Arabs prostrated themselves on the ground only before God. Harun was called the 'Shadow of God on earth', his courtiers kissed the ground when they came into his presence, and the executioner stood behind Harun's throne to show that he had the power of life and death. The first Abbasids had moved their capital to Baghdad, an old market town on the western bank of the river Tigris. By the eighth century it had become the centre of the Muslim world, and both the city and its caliphs grew hugely rich from trade and the tribute which poured through its gates.

Harun entered public life at the age of eighteen, when his father put him in charge of a raid on their traditional enemies in Byzantium. He was accompanied by his very able tutor Yahya bin Khalid the Barmaki, the father of Ja'far with whom he was later said to wander the streets of Baghdad. Their success so impressed his father that Harun was appointed successor after his elder brother Hadi. In 786 Hadi was murdered, and having ascended the throne Harun handed most of the daily administration of government to Yahya al Barmaki and his two sons, Fadl and Ja'far. Under their guidance the city grew in wealth and power. When not leading his armies in battle, Harun encouraged the study and translation of classical Greek texts on medicine, mathematics and philosophy. Harun himself is said to have been a scholar and a poet. The last years of his reign, however, were marred by the fall from power of the Barmaki

Dish stamped with couplet written in Kufic script: 'Do not abandon hope, long though the quest may endure. You will find ease of heart, if only you are patient.' Iraq, 9th century.

family. It is unclear whether Harun grew jealous of their power or genuinely believed they were plotting against him, but in 803 Ja'far was arrested and beheaded, and his father and brother imprisoned. Harun did not long survive them, dying at the age of forty-five in 807.

The dishes that I have chosen for Harun al' Rashid's feast are all traditional dishes dating back to Abbasid times but which, in some guise, are still served in Iraq today. The first essentials are large dishes of fresh herbs, salads and pickles. These are served with every Arab meal and would be ranged along the festive tables. The salad platters should include spring onions, radishes, celery and lots of fresh herbs — mint, parsley, coriander, tarragon and any other green leaves that you fancy. They should all be really fresh and just washed and shaken dry. They do not need any dressing as the pickles are used to add flavour. You can buy the pickles in most Middle Eastern shops, and you should make sure that you offer pickled cucumber, turnip, beetroot, baby aubergine (eggplant), garlic, ginger and lemon. To make your own will take a couple of weeks, as the vegetables spend one week in a solution of salt with parsley and garlic, and then a further week in vinegar which has been boiled with pepper and the 'seven spices'. Most dishes use this combination of spices, comprising black and white pepper, cinnamon, cumin, cloves, coriander and turmeric. You can make the mixture yourself, or buy it ready-mixed from most Arab or Indian food stores. You should also be able to buy dried limes, which give a quite delicious sweet-sour flavour to the recipes below.

The other essential for your feast is flat bread. Ideally it should be baked fresh in a tenour oven but I realize that this may be beyond the means of most feasters. However, from Arab or Indian shops you will be able to buy a range of flat breads, or simply buy pitta breads which can be briefly heated in a microwave and served warm in large flat baskets. Torn into manageable pieces, the bread and the leaves from the salads are used to make small parcels of the herbs and pickles which can then be eaten with the fingers. The bread can also be used to scoop up cooked foods and sauces.

Although the consumption of alcohol is strictly forbidden by the Qur'an, wines might well have been have been served at great banquets. Harun al' Rashid himself was known to be a devout Muslim so his feasts may have been 'dry', but there is a report of a banquet in the time of his son at which beautiful women formed themselves into a fountain down which wines were poured into a basin below where guests were invited to fill their glasses. However, Iraq produces such a wonderful selection of non-alcoholic drinks that you might be quite happy to serve an alcohol-free feast. Pomegranate seeds were crushed with sugar and lemon juice to make a brilliantly coloured ruby drink. Tamarind was soaked, then sweetened with sugar to create a deep golden liquid. Sheets of dried apricots were dissolved in water and then sieved, almonds were pulverized and then boiled in water and sieved, and sour yogurt was thinned with water and then served with fresh mint leaves. You will find pomegranate and tamarind syrup in Arab or Indian food shops; it can be diluted with plain or fizzy water. You can also find sheets of apricot in Arab or Indian food stores and should be able to buy ready-made almond milk in most health food stores. You can buy sour drinking yogurt in Arab or Indian stores or you can dilute plain Greek yogurt with still or fizzy water and serve it with fresh or dried mint.

Mtabbak — Rice Folded with Fish

SERVES 8

Baghdad was situated on the river Tigris, only 40 miles from the junction with the river Euphrates which, combined with it position astride the trading routes to the east, accounted for much of its prosperity as a mercantile centre. However it also meant that there was always a liberal supply of fresh fish, much of which is still cooked in riverside restaurants in the modern city. You can use any river fish for this dish, although grey mullet is the favourite.

16 tablespoons white long grain rice
6 tablespoons olive or sunflower oil
8 largish fillets of grey mullet or other river fish
1 teaspoon of 'fish spices' — ½ teaspoon ground cloves mixed with ¼ teaspoon each of
ground cumin and ground coriander
2 large onions, peeled and chopped
4 tablespoons sultanas, softened for 3 minutes in hot water
4 dried limes, pips removed and broken into small pieces
2 tablespoons flaked almonds
1 large lemon

Soak the rice for 10 minutes, then rinse and drain. Put in a large pan and cover with boiling salted water to about 25 cm /1 in above the rice. Bring to the boil, then reduce the heat and simmer for 10 minutes. Turn off the heat and cover the pan closely, using a tea cloth under the lid, and leave for 30 minutes during which it will absorb the rest of the water.

Wash, dry and salt the fish fillets, then sprinkle with some of the fish spice. Heat the oil in a pan large enough to hold the fish, and fry briskly on both sides for between 3 and 4 minutes on each side. Remove the fish from the pan and reserve.

Add the onion to the remaining oil with the rest of the fish spices and fry till golden. Add the sultanas, the dried lime and the almonds, and continue to cook briskly without burning for 4–5 minutes.

Remove half the rice from the rice pot and lay the fish fillets on top of the rest. You may need to use two pots at this stage. Spoon the onion mixture over the fish, then cover with the remains of the rice. Cover the pot closely once more and leave on a very low heat for 10–15 minutes for the flavours to infuse the rice.

Remove the upper layer of rice which will now be mixed with the onion mixture and set aside. Remove the fish fillets. Spoon the white rice from the bottom of the pot onto a serving dish. Cover this with the onion and lime rice and lay the fish over the top. Serve at once with a squeeze of lemon.

Kuzi

SERVES 8

For a great feast this dish would be made with a whole lamb, its belly filled with the rice stuffing. Huge golden platters would be covered with cooked rice, decorated with 'jewels' of golden saffron rice, sultanas and golden toasted almonds. The rice would have been the fine Ambar rice which had been grown since time immemorial by the womenfolk of the Arab marshlands of southern Iraq, now sadly drained. The nearest equivalent, although it is said not to be quite as delicious, is a good quality white Basmati rice.

1 large leg of lamb
20 tablespoons white long grain rice
16 strands saffron
5 tablespoons olive oil
1 medium onion, peeled and very finely chopped
1 tablespoon flaked or chopped almonds
½ teaspoon of 'seven spice' mix
4 tablespoon sultanas soaked in hot water for 3 minutes, then drained
salt
8 cloves garlic, peeled but left whole
1 tablespoon butter
3 tablespoons of whole skinned almonds

Amina Eating the Rice by H.J. Ford. Published in *The Arabian Nights Entertainments*, 1898.

Bone out the leg of lamb quite roughly so that you end up with quite a number of extra bits of lamb. Trim off the extra meat, chop it very small, and set aside. Reserve the bones for stock for another dish.

Put 2 tablespoons of rice in a small saucepan and cover generously with boiling water. Add 6 strands of saffron. Bring back to the boil and cook at a rolling boil for 5 minutes or until it is nearly, but not quite, cooked. Drain the rice. (An Iraqi cook would always save the nutritious rice cooking water for another dish such as soup, or as a drink for the sick or for small babies.) Heat 1 tablespoon of oil in a pan and briskly fry the reserved meat with the onion, chopped almonds and spice mix for 2–3 minutes. Add to the cooked rice along with 1 tablespoon of drained sultanas, and season lightly with salt.

Use this mixture to stuff the cavities in the lamb, then tie the lamb very thoroughly with a thin thread so that the stuffing cannot fall out. Cut 8 small slits in the lamb and insert the garlic cloves.

Heat 2 tablespoons of oil in a heavy deep pan large enough to hold the lamb.

Fry the lamb briskly on all sides until it is lightly browned all over. Add water to the pot, to about halfway up the lamb. Bring to the boil, then cover and turn the heat down really low and simmer for 45–50 minutes. Meanwhile, heat the oven to 180 C / 350 F / Gas Mark 4.

Remove the lamb from the pot. Dry it with kitchen towel, and then oil it thoroughly all over. Put the lamb in a baking tray and bake for a further 45 minutes. When you put the lamb into the oven you can start to prepare the rice.

Wash and rinse 10 tablespoons of rice well, then separate off 2 tablespoons. Heat 2 tablespoons of oil in a large pan with a lid. Add 8 tablespoons of rice and stir it gently to make sure that all the grains are coated with oil. Add half a teaspoon of salt and enough cold water to cover the rice by about 25 cm / 1 in. Bring to the boil, lower the heat and cook very gently for about 10 minutes. Stir very gently, then cover the pot tightly (you can put a tea towel beneath the lid) and leave it for 30 minutes during which it will absorb the water.

At the same time follow exactly the same procedure with the remaining 2 tablespoons of rice (this time adding only a pinch of salt), but add 10 strands of saffron to the cooking water. While the rice is cooking, use the remaining tablespoon of oil to fry the almonds until they are golden all over. Set aside. When the rice is cooked, add an appropriate size knob of butter to each pot and stir gently.

Spread the white rice out on a large tray or serving dish. Use the saffron rice, the whole almonds and the sultanas to create patterns on the rice, leaving space in the middle for the lamb. Remove the lamb from the oven. Carefully remove the threads and place in the middle of the rice.

Drawing of a pheasant design on the inside of a silver bowl from Iran, dating from the 4th or 5th century.

Threed

SERVES 8

Threed is the name given to a meat dish, usually lamb but sometimes game as here, which uses dried bread to sop up the cooking juice sauce. In this recipe I have used the breasts of 4 small game birds but you could also use 1 kilo / 2½ lbs of diced lamb. To sop up the cooking juices, the bread should be both stale and dried out in the oven.

7 tablespoons olive oil
6 medium onions, peeled and chopped finely
3 heaped teaspoons of seven spice mixture
4 small game birds
1.2 litres / 2 pints / 5 cups water
12 dried limes
4 large pieces of stale Arabic flat bread
4 tablespoons of flaked or chopped almonds

Heat 4 tablespoons of oil in a large deep pan, and briskly fry the onions and seven spice mixture for 5–10 minutes or until the onions are softening and turning golden. Add the game birds, the water and the dried limes. Bring to the boil, then reduce the heat and simmer very gently, uncovered, for 1–1½ hours. Allow to cool in the juices.

Remove the birds and remove their breasts. Reserve the bones and legs for stock or soup and return the breasts to the cooking juices. Remove the dried limes.

Cut up 4 medium-size stale Arab flat breads into small squares and dry out in a low oven for 20 minutes. Gently re-heat the breasts in the juices and heat the remaining oil. Lay the toasted bread out in the bottom of the serving dish. Pour the juices over the bread, then the oil over the juices. Lay the breasts on top, sprinkle with the almonds, and serve at once.

Rosewater Scented Rice

SERVES 8

This ground rice dessert would probably have been made with ewes' milk — and certainly can be if you can get it. It would have been served in silver or golden goblets decorated with pistachio nuts and crystallized rose petals.

1.2 litres / 2 pints / 5 cups ewes' or cows' milk
2 level tablespoons sugar
8 level tablespoons ground rice
1 level teaspoon cardamom powder
4–5 tablespoons rosewater
2 tablespoons of pistachio nuts, shelled and crushed
16 crystallized rose petals

Put the milk in a saucepan with the sugar, ground rice and cardamom powder. Bring gently to the boil, stirring continuously, and cook for a couple of minutes while it thickens. Pour into serving glasses or dishes and allow to cool and thicken slightly. Decorate with the crushed pistachio and rose petals, and serve at room temperature.

Madguga

Makes 15–20 balls or squares

Dates were said to be the gift of Allah to the Arab people as they supply the body with all it needs. The Qur'an describes them as one of the beauties of paradise. The magnificent trees provided desperately needed shade in the boiling heat of summer. The huge tough leaves could be used for anything from wrapping food to roofing houses, while the central spine of the leaves could be cut down into a spit, or bound together to make supports for a house. But most importantly, the delicious fruits were not only highly nutritious and an excellent source of sugar, but could be dried and preserved for years.

A small platter for delicacies. Four almond shapes at the corners and a small orange-sized central section suggest its intended contents. From Abbasid Egypt, 9th century.

The Madguga would have been made in a Hawan or large mortar and pestle, in which the dates could be beaten with the nuts and seeds. However, it works very well in a food processor and takes a lot less energy.

450 g / 1 lb soft dried dates, stoned
4 tablespoons shelled walnuts
4 tablespoons sesame seeds
1 teaspoon fennel seeds

Put the dates, walnuts, half the sesame seeds and the fennel seeds into the food processor and process until you have a rough paste. How smooth you wish to make it is a matter of taste, so process it as much or as little as you need. Roll the mixture into small balls or flatten on a tray and cut into squares. Roll in the extra sesame seeds and leave to dry out slightly. Serve after the meal with coffee or fresh fruits.

3

Dining at the Court of Lucrezia Borgia

Glass goblet, made in Venice at the end of the 15th century. Its elaborate decoration and portraits on either side suggest that it was a betrothal or wedding gift.

In the fearsome popular picture of Lucrezia Borgia as poisoner, murderer and incestuous lover, it is hard to recognize the 'most beautiful maiden, modest, lovable, decorous – only exceeded in beauty by her charm of manner' described by Johannes Lucas, ambassador to Duke Ercole d'Este I. As Duchess of Ferrara she was loved as much by the poor and sick of her city as by the poets and courtiers who crowded her court. The Borgia name was certainly tainted with blood – neither Lucrezia's father nor her brother hesitated to use poison or the assassin's blade to remove an unwanted rival, but there is no evidence that Lucrezia was even aware of their machinations, let alone party to their crimes.

She was born in 1480, the illegitimate daughter of Pope Alexander VI (Rodrigo Borgia). Her brother was Cesare Borgia, on whom Machiavelli based *The Prince*. Alexander saw his daughter as a useful ploy in his plans for territorial aggrandizement. In 1493, at the age of thirteen, she was married to Giovanni Sforza, a member of the powerful Sforza family in Milan. The marriage created a strong alliance against the Aragonese king of Naples. By 1496, however, Alexander had changed sides, and he had the marriage annulled by forcing Giovanni to admit to impotence. Lucrezia was bethrothed instead to the seventeen-year-old Alonso of Naples. During the bargaining over the divorce and the new betrothal, Lucrezia, now aged sixteen, was placed in a convent where she is said to have become pregnant by a young chamberlain by the name of Perotto. Furious, her brother had him killed. Cesare was later accused by the Sforza family of fathering the child himself, thus fuelling rumours of Lucrezia's incest.

Detail from *The Feast of the Gods*, begun by Giovanni Bellini and completed by Titian, 1514–29.
The painting was commissioned by Lucrezia's third husband, Alfonso d'Este,
to decorate the study of their castle in Ferrara.

Engraving of Lucrezia
Borgia after a painting
by Guercino, *c.* 1500.

Lucrezia and Alonso of Naples married and, it seems, fell deeply in love. By the time their first child was due, however, the Borgia's political allegiances were changing yet again and Alonso needed to be removed. He survived an attack by Cesare's men, nursed tenderly by the distraught Lucrezia. Not to be so easily baulked, Cesare then had his henchmen strangle Alonso to death. Lucrezia was inconsolable, and at least one poem survives in which she expresses her grief at Alonso's violent death as well as her rage with Cesare. However, her position as the closest female relative of two of the most powerful men in Renaissance Italy meant that, despite her grief and rage, she was married off again. Alonso's death cleared the way for the third and richest alliance for Lucrezia, to Alfonso d'Este, Prince of Ferrara, a city-state adjacent to Cesare's province of Romagna. This was the grandest of all Lucrezia's weddings, taking place in 1502. The recipe quoted on page 40 was said to have been created especially for the wedding feast.

For the rest of her life Lucrezia remained in Ferrara, the mother of five more children and at the centre of a court frequented by all the poets and learned men of the day. That Lucrezia was intelligent and talented was widely recognized. Aged only twenty-one, before her marriage to Alfonso d'Este, she had been left by her father in charge of the administration of the Vatican and the church while he was away from the city. In later years she successfully adminstered Ferrara on several occasions in the absence of her husband. She was a talented linguist, speaking Spanish, Italian and French, and reading some Latin and Greek.

To her deep distress Rodrigo, her son by Alonso of Naples, died in 1512 at the age of thirteen. Five years later, at the age of thirty-nine, Lucrezia died of puerperal fever after the birth of her seventh child. She was deeply mourned by her court and by the people of Ferrara, for whom she had performed many works of charity and founded hospitals and schools. Known as 'the Good Duchess' she was remembered for her golden blond hair, her good humour and gaiety, and her *dolce ciera* (her sweet face).

Although we know that Lucrezia's household was very grand we do not, sadly, have any recipes that came directly from her kitchens. However, we do have the wonderful recipes of Cristoforo di Messisbugo, Steward of the Household to Lucrezia's brother-in-law, Cardinal Ippolito d'Este. Messisbugo was responsible not only for creating elegant food for the court, but for court etiquette, the management of guests, the planning of the entertainment, and the pacing of the meal so that guests' digestions were not overloaded. His book *Libro Novo*, therefore, includes instructions as to the laying of tables, the decorations of the room, suitable entertainments and flower arrangements, as well as recipes. So successful was he in his endeavours that in 1533 he was created Count Palatine in recognition of his art. But despite the richness and sophistication of the Ferrarese court, Messisbugo's recipes are simple and have a succulent freshness to them. His instructions for the table and the planning of the menu are rather more elaborate:

FOR THE TOP TABLE THERE SHOULD BE

Candelabra of Silver

Bowls of Silver

In summer, seasonal flowers

In winter, artificial flowers in silk and in gold

A rose laid on top of each napkin

Toothpicks to clean the teeth

Dishes of breads which should be plaited

Dishes of sweet pastry boats and fried pastry crescents

Sweet wines and Greek wines

Dishes of truffles, and capers and sultanas

FIRST COURSE

Partridges

Capons

Roast meats with many sauces

Tortellini of wild boar in stock

Little roasted kids

Royal Soup with tagliatelli

Partridges in jelly

Whipped cream

Good cheeses

Bergamot pears

Cardoons

After this course there should be music and singing,
while the guests' hands are washed and the cloths are changed.

THEN SHOULD BE SERVED
Fruits in syrup
Lemons
Oranges
Quinces
Candied fruits
Morello cherries
Nougat pieces
Toothpicks should be made available for the guests
Then there should be more music played on lovely instruments.

Cristoforo Di Messisbugo's Suppa Grassa

SERVES 8

This light and simple soup, made special by the slightly startling combination of parmesan, sugar and cinnamon, is an ideal way to start a long and heavy meal.

1 small chicken
2 onions, thickly sliced
3 cloves garlic, peeled and halved
1 stalk celery
4 mushrooms, halved
1 carrot, scrubbed and sliced in thick rounds
2 sprigs parsley
2 bayleaves
2 sprigs fresh thyme or 1 heaped teaspoon dried thyme
2 litres water
300 ml / 10 floz / 1¼ cups dry white wine
300 ml / 10 floz / 1¼ cups medium sherry

Take a slice of bread and put in the oven to become like biscuit. Take some parmesan and grate it and mix it with some sugar and cinnamon and a little pepper, so that it is enough. And have some very good chicken or meat stock and put the cheese at the bottom of the dish and cover with the bread and pour over the stock and keep it hot until you bring it to the table.

34

8 small round slices of wholemeal (wholewheat) bread, crusts removed
100 g / 4 oz fresh parmesan
40 grinds of black pepper
2 heaped teaspoons light muscovado sugar
1 heaped teaspoon ground cinnamon

Put the chicken in a large pan with the onions, garlic, celery, mushrooms, carrot, parsley, bayleaves, thyme, water and white wine. Bring slowly to the boil and simmer gently for 1½ hours or until the meat is falling off the bone. Meanwhile, toast the slices of bread in a warm oven until they are biscuit crisp.

Remove the stock from the heat and strain through a fine sieve. Reserve the meat for another purpose and discard the vegetables. Re-heat the stock, season to taste and add the sherry. Keep hot but do not boil.

Grate the parmesan finely into a bowl. Grind in the fresh black pepper, add the sugar and the cinnamon, and mix well. Sprinkle the parmesan mixture over the base of a large soup tureen or into the bottom of 8 soup bowls, then cover with the slices of bread. Spoon or pour the stock over the bread and serve at once.

Italian maiolica dish, c. 1490–1525. Dishes of this type often depicted well-known and beautiful women.

Cristoforo di Messisbugo's Torta d'Herbe

SERVES 8

'Take washed spinach and put it in a pot and throw in oil and fry it well and chop it and put it in a pot with sugar and cinnamon and pepper and raisins and figs, cut thin, and sultanas and peeled walnuts and mix everything together well. And then you will prepare your case and you will cook it following the order for a lenten pie.'

Although this recipe is for a 'lenten pie' it can be served as part of your first course and will be a pleasant alternative to the meats. The combination of dried fruits and nuts with the vegetables is a strong hangover from the Middle Ages.

50 g / 2 oz light muscovado sugar
¼ teaspoon powdered saffron or 10 saffron strands
300 g / 10 oz wholemeal (stoneground) flour
140 g / 5 oz butter
3 egg yolks
2–3 tablespoons rosewater
1 heaped tablespoon raisins
1 heaped tablespoon sultanas
2 kilo / 4 lb fresh spinach or 900 g / 2 lb cooked or frozen spinach
salt and pepper
5 tablespoons olive oil
40 g / 1½ oz walnut kernels
4 fresh or dried figs
1 tablespoon pale muscovado sugar
½ teaspoon ground cinnamon
1 teaspoon ground nutmeg (freshly ground if possible)
2 tablespoons dried breadcrumbs
1 tablespoon milk

Pound the sugar and saffron together, then mix into the flour. Rub in the butter, and mix in 2 egg yolks and the rosewater. Form the pastry into a ball but do not knead or it will become tough. Chill the dough for at least 30 minutes.

Soak the fried fruit, if it needs it, in boiling water for 5 minutes then drain and dry thoroughly.

Trim, wash, and cook the fresh spinach without putting any water in the pan,

Salt-cellar designs by Giulio Romano. Italian, 1530s. The clear outlines would have provided a simple guide for the goldsmith.

or defrost and drain the frozen spinach. Add 1 scant teaspoon of salt. When the spinach is tender, drain, and once cool enough, squeeze it between your hands.

Heat the olive oil in a wide pan and sauté the spinach gently in the oil for 10 minutes, stirring frequently so that it takes up the flavour. Chop it coarsely and transfer to a bowl. Blanch the walnuts for 20 seconds in boiling water. Drain and rub off as much of the bitter skin as you can. Chop the kernels with the figs and add them to the spinach. Add the sultanas and raisins, the sugar, cinnamon and nutmeg, and season with salt and pepper. Mix very thoroughly.

Heat the oven to 190 C / 375 F / Gas Mark 5. Roll out the pastry so that you can cut out two 25 cm / 8 in diameter discs (for the bottom and top of the pie), and strips wide enough to line the sides. Use a pastry disc to line the bottom and sides of a 25 cm / 8 in springform tin. Sprinkle the bottom with the dried breadcrumbs, then spoon the spinach mixture into the tin and cover with the other pastry disc. Use the pastry scraps to decorate the pie.

Mix the remaining egg yolk with the milk and use to seal the edges and glaze the top of the pie. Bake the pie for 30 minutes, then reduce the heat to 180 C / 350 F / Gas Mark 4 and bake for a further 10 minutes until the pastry is golden brown.

The pie should be served warm or at room temperature, so allow to cool before removing from the tin onto a serving dish.

Cristoforo di Messisbugo's Fraccassea Inglese Sopra Strurione O Manzo, O Vitello, or Castrone

SERVES 8

The meat should be roasted or boiled. Take bitter orange and lemon, cinnamon and pepper and a few cloves and a pinch of ginger and moisten with egg yolk according to the quantities that you have to make. Replace the meat in the pan with the sauce and make it hot and bring it to the table flavoured with fennel seeds.

By cooking the meat at least a day ahead, the flavours will have time to develop. Cooking it in advance will also allow you to remove the fat from the top.

4 tablespoons olive oil
2 onions, peeled and chopped very small
2 sticks celery, chopped very small
4 cloves garlic, peeled and chopped very small
8 mushrooms, wiped and chopped small
1 teaspoon ground cinnamon and 10 cloves
2 kilo / 4½ lb joint of beef (brisket or topside), loin of veal, venison or buffalo, rolled and tied
1 wine glass Marsala
500 ml stock / 18 fl oz / 2¼ cups
3 egg yolks
1½ teaspoons each ground cinnamon & ground ginger
1–2 tablespoons cider vinegar
sea salt and freshly ground black pepper
1 heaped teaspoon fennel seeds

Heat the oil in a heavy, deep pan, large enough to hold the meat. Add the onions, celery, garlic, mushrooms, cinnamon and cloves. Cook gently for 15–20 minutes or until the onion is soft. Place the rolled meat on top, pour over the Marsala and the stock. Cover the pan, bring gently to the boil and simmer for 2–3 hours. Allow to cool, then chill so that the fat rises to the top. When cold, discard the fat.

To serve, re-heat the meat gently in the stock. Meanwhile, mix the egg yolks with the cinnamon, ginger and 1 tablespoon of cider vinegar. Gradually add 300 ml of the stock, strained. Pour into a small saucepan and heat very gradually, stirring frequently, until the sauce amalgamates and thickens slightly. Season to taste with salt and pepper and extra vinegar if you fancy it. Remove the meat from the stock, slice it thickly and lay on a warmed serving dish. In the original recipe the sauce was served as a side dish. You may prefer to spoon the sauce over the meat.

Cristoforo di Messisbugo's Pesce a Cappucciolo

SERVES 8

Like the dish above the fish would have been served on its own, but it would be fine to add vegetables or a salad.

2 medium sized sea bass or bream, each big enough to serve 4 people
2 tablespoons coriander or fennel seeds
2 teaspoons salt
6 tablespoons white wine vinegar
6 tablespoons dry white wine
1 tablespoon melted butter
4 hard-boiled egg yolks
100 g / 4 oz walnuts
50 g / 2 oz sultanas
1 heaped teaspoon light muscovado sugar
1 teaspoon honey
8 sprigs fresh parsley
1 teaspoon sea salt
2 teaspoons dried mint or 4 teaspoons chopped fresh mint
2 tablespoons cider vinegar
300 ml / 10 fl oz / 1¼ cups
2 tablespoons wholemeal (stone ground) flour

Carefully gut and remove the backbone from the fish. To be authentic, the fish would be cut down the backbone to remove the bone and guts. You would leave both head and tail attached to the skin, and lay the fish out in a large flat dish.

Bruise the coriander or fennel seeds thoroughly with a rolling pin in a small bowl, then add the salt, white wine and white wine vinegar, and pour this mixture

'There are a great variety of fish that are good to be cooked this way. Take the fish and open it from the back and take out the guts. Soak it in vinegar and wine and salt and coriander or fennel seeds, well pounded. Leave in the marinade for 3–4 hours but no longer.

Then wash it and dry it and flour it very lightly and then put it on the spit (threaded or tied) and cook turning around with the skewer from one side to another.

You take some cleaned walnuts, hard boiled egg yolks, sultanas, honey and sugar, parsley and mint and pound well, dampening with some verjuice and you will strain it through the sieve and you will boil it just enough to thicken it.

When you want to serve the fish you will put this mixture on top and so serve.'

over the fish. Cover the fish and set it aside to marinate for 3–4 hours only. Meanwhile, put the egg yolks, walnuts, sultanas, sugar, honey, parsley, mint, salt and vinegar in a food processor and purée. Turn into a small saucepan and add the hot water. Cook this mixture very gently for 10–15 minutes to amalgamate the flavours, then spoon into a bowl.

Take the fish out of the marinade, rinse it, dry it, and flour it lightly in wholewheat flour. If you have a spit you could lash the fish onto the spit, brush it with melted butter, and roast it for 10–15 minutes. Alternatively, place on a grill pan, brush with the melted butter, and grill for 5–10 minutes on each side. Fold the fish back into a fish shape, lay on a serving platter and dish the sauce separately.

Torta Tagliarini de Ferrara

SERVES 8

Still served in Ferrara today, this traditional tart was said to have been created for Lucrezia's wedding feast in 1502. The tangled topping of golden pasta represents her golden blond hair.

A couple about to dance at a banquet. From a manuscript, *c.* 1520.

150 g / 6 oz wholemeal (stoneground) flour
50 g / 2 oz light muscovado sugar
100 g / 4 oz cold butter
5 egg yolks
juice of ½ lemon
50 g / 2 oz fresh tagliarini or cappellini or 75 g / 3 oz dried
150 g / 6 oz blanched almonds, lightly browned in a low oven
125 g / 4½ oz light muscovado sugar
1 tablespoon wholemeal (stoneground) flour
6 tablespoons unsalted butter, melted
½ teaspoon of almond essence
2 tablespoons Galliano or liqueur of Moscato
3 tablespoons water

In a large bowl mix the flour and sugar. Cut and rub the butter into the flour. Beat 2 egg yolks with the lemon juice and 1 tablespoon of cold water. Lightly mix into the flour and butter and form into a ball. Sprinkle with extra water if too dry but do not knead or the pastry will become tough. Chill.

Heat the oven to 190 C / 375 F / Gas Mark 5. Rub the inside of a 24 cm / 9 in flan dish with a little oil. If you do not want to serve the tart in the flan dish, use a metal dish with a removable bottom. Press the paste out over the base and up the sides of the tin. Line the paste with foil and weight with beans. Bake for 10 minutes (13 minutes if in a ceramic dish), then remove the foil and beans and bake for a further 8 minutes. Remove from the oven.

Bring a saucepan of lightly salted water to the boil and blanch the pasta – for no more than 10 seconds for fresh pasta and 1 minute for dried. Rinse under cold water, then drain and spread on paper towels to dry.

Coarsely chop a quarter of the almonds and set aside. Pulverize the remaining almonds with the sugar and flour in the processor. Add the melted butter, the almond essence, liqueur, water and 3 egg yolks, and purée. Pour the almond mixture into the pie shell. Distribute the pasta over the mixture and press lightly down into it so that it is partially submerged. Sprinkle over the remaining almonds. Bake for 35 minutes at 180 C / 350 F / Gas Mark 4.

4

Hiawatha's Wedding Feast

Today Henry Wadsworth Longfellow's *Song of Hiawatha* evokes little more than a smile, yet when it was published in 1855, 5000 copies were sold in the first five weeks. Longfellow's lilting romance told the tale of the Indian prophet and deliverer Hiawatha, dispatched by the Great Spirit to guide the nations. The character of Hiawatha himself was loosely based on the semi-historical founder of the Iroquois Federation. But although Longfellow instinctively understood the intimate bond between the Indian and the land which fed and nurtured him, his Hiawatha was a much glamorized, and indeed sanitized, portrait of the original Indian chief.

In Longfellow's tale, Hiawatha grows to manhood under the tender care of his grandmother 'old Nokomis', who teaches him the ways of the birds and the beasts.

He learns that his mother had died of a broken heart when abandoned by his father Mudkejeewis, the West Wind. The first trial of his manhood is to travel to the kingdom of the West Wind to confront and defeat his father. Victory over the magician Megissogwon, the Pearl Feather follows.

In canto five, Hiawatha retires to the forest to fast and to seek wisdom in how he can better the lot of his people. He lists the foods that the forests and rivers provide for his tribe:

Iroquois chief wearing a feathered headdress, illustrating the *Song of Hiawatha*. Postcard from 1905.

The Manner of Their Fishing by John White. The artist was one of a group of English settlers who arrived on the east coast of North America in 1585. He depicts three fishing methods – a dip net and spear; a fire in a canoe to attract fish at night; and weirs to trap the fish.

Henry Wadsworth
Longfellow. From
the 19th-century
publication *National
Portrait Gallery*, vol. 2,
p. 445.

On the first day of his fasting
Through the leafy woods he wandered;
Saw the deer start from the thicket,
Saw the rabbit in his burrow,
Heard the pheasant, Bena, drumming,
Heard the squirrel, Adjidaumo,
Rattling in his hoard of acorns,
Saw the Pigeon, the Omeme,
Building nests among the pine trees,
And in flocks the wild goose, Wawa,
Flying to the fenlands northward,
Whirring, wailing far above him...

On the next day of his fasting
By the river's brink he wandered
Through the Muskoday, the Meadow,
Saw the wild rice, Mahnomonee,

Saw the blueberry, Meenahga,
And the strawberry, Odahmin,
And the gooseberry, Shahbomin,
And the grape-vine, the Bemaghut,
Trailing o'er the alder branches...

On the third day of his fasting
By the lake he sat and pondered,
By the still transparent water;
Saw the sturgeon, Nahma, leaping,
Scattering drops like beads of wampum,
Saw the yellow perch, the Sahwa,
Like a sunbeam on the water,
Saw the pike, the Maskenozha,
And the herring, Okahahwis,
And the Shawgashee, the crawfish!

The tenth canto of Longfellow's *Song of Hiawatha* describes his wooing of Minehaha, Laughing Water, the daughter of the ancient arrow maker, 'in the land of the Dacotahs'. Hiawatha first saw her on his way back from his encounter with his father and despite his grandmother's pleas to pick a bride from his own tribe, Hiawatha's heart is already lost. Suggesting that the union will also secure peace between their tribes, Hiawatha asks the ancient arrow maker for his daughter's hand. The most benevolent of fathers, the arrow maker

Looked at Hiawatha proudly,
Fondly looked at Laughing Water,
And made answer, very gravely:
Yes, if Minehaha wishes...

Despite her misgivings, on the happy couple's arrival old Nokomis sets to prepare the wedding feast.

The foods listed as Hiawatha fasts in the forest is a fairly comprehensive list of what would have been available to old Nokomis, although Hiawatha does not mention either the wide range of North American nuts or the syrup from the maple tree. Nor does he mention the corn which sprung from his friend Mondamin's grave and which formed such a vital part of the American diet — especially when combined with beans and squash into the famous 'Three Sisters'. Nonetheless old Nokomis had plenty to choose from, and the feast that she made sounds pretty appealing:

Sumptuous was the feast Nokomis
Made at Hiawatha's wedding.
All the bowls were made of bass-wood,
White and polished very smoothly,
All the spoons of horn of bison,
Black and polished very smoothly

First they ate the sturgeon, Nahma,
And the pike, the Maskenozha,
Caught and cooked by old Nokomis.
Then on pemmican they feasted,

Pemmican and buffalo marrow,
Haunch of deer and hump of bison,
Yellow cakes of the Mondamin,
And the wild rice of the river.

But the gracious Hiawatha,
And the lovely Laughing Water,
And the careful old Nokomis,
Tasted not the food before them,
Only waited on the others,
Only served their guests in silence.

Delightful though Longfellow's picture of Hiawatha's feast may be, one should remember that Longfellow's spectacles were heavily tinted with rose. In this extract from a pamphlet published in 1853 'by a Fur Trader' on the 'Traits of American

Three Iroquois Indians by George Catlin, 1861–69.

Indian Life', hostly abstinence appears to have been the norm, but that is about where the resemblance ends:

> At length the important business of the day commenced ... and Hannaya (the chief) advanced and laid before me a beaver. Then returning to his store where were piled huge heaps of dried meats, with vessels of bear's grease and fish oil, besides quantities of berry cakes, seized another beaver and, squatting down in front of the most dignified of his native guests, presented it to him tail foremost. Upon this the honoured individual seized a knife, and commenced forthwith an attack upon the proffered morsel which the chief continued to hold with exemplary patience until the guest had satisfied his voracity. The animal, thus despoiled of his fair proportions, was presented to another and yet another guest, the allotted portion always diminishing with the rank or consideration in which he might be held. When all were thus served, a new course, attended with like ceremonies, at once began. About a dozen of his relations assisted the head man in the distribution of the viands, the etiquette being scrupulously observed by the whole. As the banquet proceeded I observed that the guests had amassed a large heap of meats, all tossed higgledy-piggledy onto their dishes, together with a heterogenous compound of berries, bear's grease and fish oil ...'

I would not suggest that you piled all your Hiawathan dinner upon one plate – nor that the hosts should remain hungry while the guests tuck in. The bear's grease and fish oils, which do sound rather unappealing, were used as we use lard or bacon fat, to baste and lubricate the other foods. Sadly both sturgeon and pike are very hard to find, so I suggest that you use the more homely herring. Although there is no dessert listed in Haiwatha's wedding menu I have included a cake made with the berries and nuts which formed so large a part of the Iroquois diet. The cake might well have been washed down with a juice made from wild strawberries in season.

Smoked, Planked or Grilled Fish

SERVES 10

The Iroquois hung the fish over a wood fire to smoke them or, if they were too large, split them open and nailed them to a plank of wood (thus 'planked') which could be stood by the fire. Alternatively they could be grilled over an open fire — a barbecue would be ideal. If none of these options is available, the fish can be cooked on a very hot griddle or under a hot grill. The Atlantic herring, caught from the Bay of Biscay to Chesapeake Bay, can grow to 40 cm (16 in) in length, but the majority are around 20 cm / 5 in. If you would rather, you could also use a small salmon trout or a side of salmon.

5 good size herring, cleaned and split open but with the heads left on
3 tablespoons maple syrup
5 spring or green onions, chopped very finely
1 heaped teaspoon dried sage
1 teaspoon sea salt
1 tablespoon corn oil

Mix the syrup, onions, sage, salt and oil together and rub the mixture thoroughly into the fish. Cover and leave in a larder or refrigerator for 1–2 hours.

If you are smoking your fish, tie a piece of string through the gills so that you can hang them above the fire. For smoking or barbecuing your fish, ensure that the fire has burnt well down before starting to smoke. The fish will need about an hour's smoking and should be served warm with fresh watercress.

If you plan to griddle or grill the fish, lay them out on your griddle or grill pan and dribble over a little more oil. Cook for 5–10 minutes depending on the heat of your grill or griddle, but make sure that they do not burn. Serve with fresh watercress.

Roast Haunch of Venison with 'Spring Greens'

SERVES 10

Deer were plentiful throughout the northeast of America and were a common food. The Indians believed that when they ate the flesh of brave animals some of the animal's courage was transferred to the eater, so deer was a popular food. The liver and kidneys of the animals were regarded as a source of instant energy and, since they could be eaten raw, were sometimes used as a 'pick me up' after a long hunt. Because they were so nourishing and easy to heat, the remains would be taken back to the camp as a gift for the elderly.

The flesh would have been tougher than most of the farmed venison we can buy today, so it would have needed the acidity of the cranberries, vinegar and syrup in the marinade to break down the sinews. Originally the joint would have been basted with bear's grease, but by 1800 salt pork and bacon, brought to America by the settlers, had become a common ingredient in Indian food, so you would be committing no historical offence in using bacon. Maple sugar was boiled down from the sap in the sugar maple, which grows from Alabama to Lake Superior, so that it could be stored as sugar cakes. It was a long, slow process. Indian tribes used not only the roots and seeds of wild plants for food and medicine, but would boil the young leaves to eat with meat. You can use any combination of young greens to serve with the venison.

Indians using deerskins to hunt other deer. Plate XXV from *America.-Part II.-Latin*, by Theodore de Bry, 1591.

150 g / 6½ oz fresh cranberries
1 heaped teaspoon ground allspice or 2 teaspoons allspice berries
120 ml / 4 fl oz / ½ cup maple syrup
120 ml / 4 fl oz / ½ cup red wine vinegar
2 kilo / 4½ lb joint of venison
6–8 streaky bacon rashers
1 kilo / 2 lb young greens (spinach, watercress, pak choi, lettuce, parsley, chard or any combination thereof), washed, roughly dried and chopped

Lightly crush the cranberries with the allspice, maple syrup and wine vinegar in a food processor. Put the venison into a bowl large enough to hold it, and pour over the cranberry mixture, making sure that all the venison is covered. Cover and leave in a cool larder or the top of a fridge for at least 24 hours.

Heat the oven to 170 C / 325 F / Gas Mark 3. Transfer the venison to a roasting tin and pour the marinade around the bottom. Cover the joint with the bacon rashers and a piece of aluminium baking foil. Bake for 2–2½ hours, removing the foil about an hour before it is cooked. Serve with the juices. Just before you are ready to serve the venison, boil the prepared 'greens' for a couple of minutes in a few centimeters (1 in) of water. They should be little more than wilted. Serve with the venison.

Cornmeal Mush

SERVES 10

Partly because of its flexibility, corn was a staple food for most Indian peoples, and many festivals revolved around its growing season. The yellow corn that we eat today is a hybridized version of sweet corn, but until the early 1900s corn-on-the-cob was green or immature. The Iroquois grew mainly a white corn, which is still available in the northeastern states. Chicos were dried and unhulled whole corn kernels, reconstituted by soaking and then boiling until tender. Hominy was – and is – fresh or dried corn kernels which have been soaked or boiled with hardwood ashes, unslaked lime or caustic soda to remove the tough outer hulls. The rinsed

An Indian market
scene, 1595. Goods
are being traded
near the port of
Carthagena, probably
in what is now
Colombia. Plate X
from the accounts of
Girolamo Benzoni.

kernels can be ground and cooked immediately, or dried and stored until needed.
The well-known grits are hominy which has been ground into a coarse meal then
used to make a porridge-type dish. Masa and masa harina (dried masa) is meal
made from grinding wet hominy to make the tortillas and tamales of the south-
west. Parched corn is whole corn kernels which have been toasted or roasted. It
too is reconstituted by soaking, then boiling until tender.

1 litre / 1¾ pints / 4¼ cups water
2 tablespoons maple syrup
1 tablespoon dried sage
200 g / 7 oz course ground cornmeal or coarse polenta
1–2 heaped teaspoons salt

In a large saucepan bring the water to boil, reduce to a simmer and add the
maple syrup and the sage. Slowly sprinkle the cornmeal over the water, stirring

continuously to prevent it lumping. Bring back to the simmer and cook for 5 minutes. Season to taste with the salt, and serve with the venison. You can make the dish in advance and re-heat it when needed. It takes about 4 minutes in a microwave on a high setting.

Chippewa Wild Rice

SERVES 10

The highly nutritious wild rice, which appears at Hiawatha's wedding feast, was the staple food of the Chippewa Indians who lived around the Great Lakes. Wild rice was cooked with every kind of accompaniment — meat, fish, herbs, nuts and fruit. The small, skinny wild turkeys, distant ancestors of the plump birds who grace our Thanksgiving and Christmas tables, would have given excellent flavour to a dish of wild rice, as would the bone marrow (even if not buffalo bone marrow) which was served at Hiawatha's feast. I used a cock pheasant for this recipe, being the closest, relatively easily obtainable alternative to a wild turkey. The wild rice does not, unlike ordinary rice, expand at all in the cooking. It makes an excellent course in Hiawatha's feast, but is also very good on its own.

1 pheasant with the breasts removed and reserved for another dish
1 litre / 1¾ pints / 4¼ cups water
10 green spring onions or scallions, topped tailed and left whole
1 tablespoon maple syrup
large handful of watercress, chopped roughly
25 g / 1 oz blueberries
4 button mushrooms, halved
½ teaspoon salt
350 g / 14 oz wild rice

Put the pheasant into a large pot with the water, the scallions, maple syrup, watercress, blueberries, mushrooms and salt. Bring to the boil. Skim any scum from the top and simmer for 45 minutes. Remove the pheasant from the pot and carefully remove any meat from the carcass. Return the meat to the stock pot and throw out the bones and carcass. Add the wild rice to the pot, return to the boil and simmer for 40–50 minutes or until the rice is cooked. Adjust the seasoning to taste and serve with the venison and cornmush.

Strawberry Bread-cake

SERVES 10

The strawberry festival at the height of the strawberry season is one of the most important of the Iroquois' celebrations. The luscious wild strawberries were used in many dishes, including a drink made from strawberry juice thinned with water and a strawberry jelly. Hazelnut trees grew wild throughout the northeast and the nuts were widely used, both raw and roasted. This cake combines 4 favourite Iroquois ingredients – strawberries, hazelnuts, maple sugar and corn – so it will make an acceptable addition to Hiawatha's wedding meal.

250 g / 9 oz hazelnuts
200 g / 7 oz coarse cornmeal or coarse polenta
100 g / 4 oz unsalted butter
180 ml / 6 fl oz / ¾ cup maple syrup
200 g / 7 oz fresh strawberries, wild if possible
3 eggs
400 g / 14 oz mixed berries – strawberries, blueberries, gooseberries, cranberries
or whatever else you can find
maple syrup to taste

Heat the oven to 180 C / 350 F / Gas Mark 4. In a food processor, grind the hazelnuts until they are almost powdered but do not allow them to become paste. Spread them over a baking tray and roast them until they are lightly bronzed all over. Turn into a large bowl. Add the cornmeal and mix well. Melt the butter with the maple syrup and add to the mixture. Purée the strawberries in a food processor and add to the nuts and cornmeal.

You can then either beat the eggs lightly together and add them to the mixture, or separate them, beat in the yolks, and then whisk the white until stiff and fold them in. This will give you a lighter cake, although it is unlikely that old Nokomis would have given them that treatment.

Spoon into a well-greased and lined 20 cm / 8 in cake tin. Bake for 50 minutes or until a skewer comes out clean. Turn out the cake and cool on a cake rack.

Meanwhile purée the berries in a food processor and sweeten to taste with maple syrup. How much you need will depend entirely on what berries you use and how sweet you want them.

Serve the cake with the berry purée. Excellent cold, it is even more delicious served slightly warm.

A Festive Dance by John White, *c.* 1585–93. This is probably the Green Corn or Harvest Festival, to celebrate the first maize harvest at the end of summer.

10

5

Banqueting with Mughal Emperors

Say 'Mongol' and most people think of Gengis Kahn and Tamburlaine, of murderous hordes descending from the north. Say 'Mughal' and the same people will imagine fabulous wealth, the Koh-i-noor diamond and the broken-hearted Shah Jahan creating the world's most famous tomb for his dead wife. Yet the line which joins the fearsome Mongol conquerors to the most gorgeous of monarchs was not just one of direct blood descent. The passion for architecture which fired Shah Jahan had inspired Tamburlaine to bring architects from across the known world to beautify his capital, Samarkand. The love of the gardens with which Tamburlaine surrounded his towers at Samarkand was inherited by Babur who lies buried in the terraces he built at Kabul. The passion for the written word which caused Tamburlaine to assemble painters and calligraphers from the lands that he had conquered inspired his descendants to create some of the most beautiful and extensive libraries the world has known, and to chronicle their own lives, loves and times in some of the most delightful and intimate 'diaries' ever penned by royalty.

Time, however, did mellow the Timurid princes. The great Mughal emperors were still capable of mass slaughter, gruesome revenge and bouts of fratricide which would put the Borgias to shame, but in the context of their time they were liberal, enlightened and intelligent rulers. Technically, the Mughal empire lasted from 1526 until 1857, but its greatest days were over by the time that Shah Jahan was co-ordinating plans for the Taj Mahal. The practice by which sons divided the inheritance of their father, which had caused much grief and bloodshed in the early

Jade and gold *huqqa* base, *c.* 1700. Smoked at the end of lavish banquets, a *huqqa* pipe would have been attached to this very elaborate base.

A detail from *Humayun's Garden Party* by Mir Sayyid Ali, *c.* 1550–55.
The picture includes servants with trays of food and drink.

days of the empire, was to tear it apart in the eighteenth and nineteenth centuries.

Shah Jahan is by far the best-known of the Mughal emperors, but with the exception of his deeply touching devotion to his wife he is probably the least interesting. His father Jahangir was a great patron of the arts, a keen naturalist and a frank and charming diarist, but for most of his reign was ruled from the harem by his formidable wife, Nur Jahan, and suffered from the family's addiction to both alcohol and drugs. It is to Jahangir's father Akbar, who reigned from 1556 to 1605, that credit for the rise of the Mughal empire should really go. Yet despite his pivotal role in establishing the empire's efficient administration, its liberal religious policies, its huge wealth, its dramatic architecture, its skilled painters and its wonderful libraries, Akbar himself was illiterate (his early life was spent campaigning against rival claimants to his throne). His father Humayun was cultured and well-meaning, but also spent much of his reign defending his throne. The empire that he had inherited in 1530 was a fragile creation of only four years standing, much of which had been held together by the personal charisma of his father, Babur.

The first Mughal emperor of India – and the first royal diarist – Babur was a direct descendant of both Gengis Kahn and Tamburlaine, with a lasting passion for their great city of Samarkand. Despite his royal blood, his teens were spent roving the family's territories in search of a throne to occupy. Twice successful in capturing Samarkand, twice he was forced to retreat until finally, in 1504, he turned his attention to the all but vacant throne of Kabul. Having overcome token resistance, he was delighted to discover a well-fortified and international city, the hub of a busy trade network linking Persia with India, Iraq, Turkey and China, good grazing, a benign climate, excellent fruit and honey and, best of all, pleasant gardens well-watered by springs and a canal. Still only twenty-one, the prince settled in Kabul and encouraged agriculture, introduced bananas and sugar cane, and extended the gardens on the hillsides. In 1511 he made one last, but again unsuccessful, attempt to regain Samarkand. For the rest of his life he concentrated his efforts on regaining Hindustan, the kingdom which had been briefly held by Tamburlaine in 1399. His final foray into India brought him, in 1526, to Delhi, where he was proclaimed Emperor of Hindustan.

By 1528 Babur was so well-established in India that a magnificent celebration feast was held. More important guests were seated in a large semicircle, with

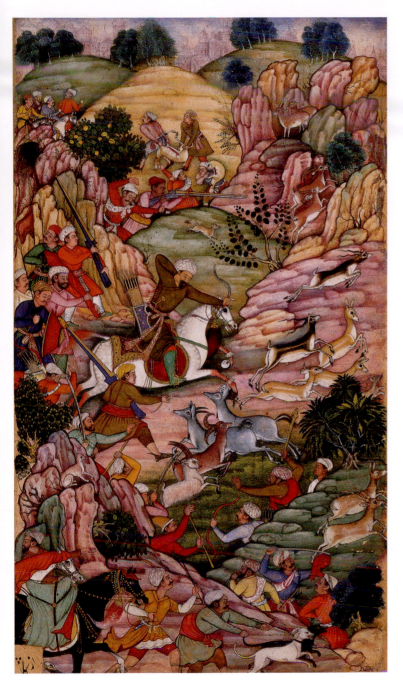

Babur in a pavilion in the centre erected for the event. Gold and silver were poured by his guests onto a carpet especially placed there for the purpose, while the emperor in turn gave gifts to his guests.

Although only forty when he became emperor, Babur was not to enjoy his new wealth for long. His early hardships, combined with his family's taste for drink and drugs, took their toll and he suffered ever more frequent bouts of illness. Only four years later Babur was dead, leaving an insecure throne but a legacy of culture and tolerance which influenced his descendants for the next five generations.

The modern cooking of northern India springs straight from the great kitchens of Babur, Jahangir and Shan Jahan – the delicate but complex spicing, the rich, creamy textures and the exotic decorations. Feasts were intended to impress, both by their quantity and by their complexity. Dishes were not served in courses in the European way. Instead a profusion of dishes was laid out on

Painting of Babur hunting deer near Kabul, Afghanistan, 1520.

beautiful carpets, along with flat breads, bowls of pickles and the bowls of flavoured yogurt or raita without which no Mughal meal would be complete. From these guests could pick and choose as their fancy took them.

Although the techniques are quite simple, the subtlety of the flavours depends not only on the spices themselves but on how they are handled. Roasting and frying brings out flavours and aromas otherwise quite lost, while frying onions to maximize the complex nuances of light and deeply browned or crisped slithers becomes an art in itself. Although these processes are not particularly difficult, they are time consuming, so do not embark on a Mughal feast unless you have a good two days to devote to shopping and preparation. If you want to understand some of the techniques and ingredients more fully, Julie Sahni's *Classic Indian Cooking* is a mine of easy-to-grasp information. For more specific instruction on the cooking of the Mughal courts, try Joyce Westrip's book, *Mughal Cooking: India's Courtly Cuisine*. Born and brought up in India, and now living in Australia, Joyce has spent years studying and researching the food of the Mughal emperors. Because of the complexity of the spicing I have quoted three of her recipes below. Do not be put off by their length, as they require time and organization rather than great expertise.

Indian woman holding a flask and glass, 1635.

Any good Indian cookbook will give you recipes for ghee and garam masala, neither of which take very long to make. Alternatively you can substitute vegetable oil for ghee and a bought garam masala for homemade.

The yogurt used in the recipes and served separately in bowls should be a thick, full-fat yogurt — Greek style will do very well. This can be served plain, or lightly flavoured with chopped fresh mint, cucumber, or almost any vegetable of your choice. A wide range of pickles to serve with your feast can be bought at any Indian food shop.

Despite the ecumenical outlook and the dipsomaniac tendencies of most of the great Mughal emperors they were at least nominally Muslim, so the most appropriate drinks to serve with your feast would be alcohol-free lassi (yogurt lightly whisked and diluted with either plain or fizzy water to taste) or fruit sherbets. You can buy a range of excellent fruit syrups in Indian food shops, which should be well-iced and diluted to taste.

Shahi Raan – Marinated Leg of Lamb
(Joyce Westrip)

SERVES 8

You need to start preparing the lamb the day before in order to allow for overnight marination. The parchment-like outer skin and all the surface fat are removed so that the full flavours of the marinade penetrate the flesh.

3½ kilo / 7 lb leg of lamb with the bone cut close to the meat

PASTE
2 roughly chopped onions

3 teaspoons roughly chopped garlic

3 tablespoons roughly chopped fresh ginger

3 fresh green chillis

1 teaspoon ground black pepper

½ teaspoon cardamom powder

3 teaspoons coriander powder

2 teaspoons cumin powder

1 teaspoon turmeric powder

¼ teaspoon mace powder

¼ teaspoon nutmeg powder

1 tablespoon almonds

1 tablespoon cashew nuts

1 tablespoon poppy seeds

1½ teaspoons salt

3 tablespoons lime or lemon juice

2 tablespoons water

MARINADE
360 ml / 12 fl oz / 1½ cups lightly whisked thick Greek yogurt

½ teaspoon saffron strands, steeped for 15 minutes in 1 tablespoon hot milk

FOR THE MEAT
2 tablespoons raisins

1 tablespoon honey

2 tablespoons melted ghee (or vegetable oil)

1 teaspoon garam masala

FOR THE GARNISH
approx 15 large onion rings

90 ml / 3 fl oz / ⅜ cup water, coloured red with beetroot or cochineal

rose petals and roasted almonds

2 tablespoons of yogurt or cream

240 ml / 8 fl oz / 1 cup stock or water

90 ml / 3 fl oz / ⅜ cup water, coloured with 2 teaspoons of turmeric powder

Trim off the parchment-like covering and all surface fat from the lamb and, if convenient, cut off the protruding bone as close to the meat as possible and set aside.

Blend all the ingredients for the paste together in a food processor. Divide into two portions and set aside.

For the marinade, combine the yogurt with the saffron threads and milk. Stir in half of the blended paste and set aside for 1 hour so that all the flavours become well integrated.

Start preparing the meat for the two stage marination. Make 3–4 deep diagonal slits across the rounded side of the flesh. Push and rub the remaining paste into these slits. Push a few raisins into each slit and set the lamb aside in a dish which can be covered for baking. Spoon the yogurt and marinade paste into the slits and spread all over the meat. Leave in this marinade for 4–6 hours or cover and refrigerate overnight. If convenient, turn the lamb and spoon over the marinade during this time.

Pre-heat the oven to 210 C / 410 F / Gas Mark 6. With the rounded (top) side face-up, dribble the honey and melted ghee over the meat. Sprinkle with the garam masala. Cover the baking dish and bake the lamb for 30 minutes, basting occasionally. Then reduce the heat to moderate, and bake until the lamb is cooked through to your liking (1½–1¾ hours), basting from time to time. Lift out of the juices on to a flat carving dish or platter.

GARNISH

While the meat is cooking divide the onion rings into 3 portions. Colour one portion red by dipping in beetroot juice or in a small bowl of water coloured with cochineal or vegetable colouring; colour the second portion yellow by soaking in a bowl of water containing 2 teaspoons of turmeric powder. Leave the third portion natural. Use these to decorate the edge of the serving platter, placing a roasted almond in the centre of each and decorating further with the rose petals.

Add the yogurt or cream and stock or water to the juices in the baking dish, and stir and simmer over a medium heat until it reaches sauce consistency. Pour into a separate sauceboat.

Carve the lamb at the table and serve with the sauce.

Shah Jahani Biryani
(Joyce Westrip)

SERVES 8

Assemble the ingredients on individual trays to represent the separate stages. You will need two heavy bottomed saucepans with close-fitting lids, and a casserole dish with a tight-fitting lid. When the chicken is underway, start the rice stage to speed things up. Allow 1 hour for the rice to soak and drain.

Mughal woman holding *pan* (type of bread), 17th century.

FOR THE CHICKEN
2 roughly chopped medium onions
2 teaspoons roughly chopped fresh ginger
1 teaspoon roughly chopped garlic
2 tablespoons blanched almonds
1 tablespoon white poppy seeds
3 tablespoons water
5 tablespoons ghee
1 teaspoon fennel seeds
2.5 cm / 1 in cinnamon stick
4 cloves
¼ teaspoon cardamom powder
1 teaspoon cumin powder
1 teaspoon coriander powder
1 teaspoon chilli powder
¼ teaspoon nutmeg powder
¼ teaspoon mace powder
1 teaspoon garam masala
375 g / 13 oz skinned chicken breast or thigh fillets, cut into large bite-size pieces
1½ teaspoons salt
1 tablespoon seedless raisins
3 tablespoons lightly whisked yogurt

¼ teaspoon saffron strands steeped for 15 minutes in 1 tablespoon hot milk

FOR THE AROMATIC RICE
225 g / 8 oz basmati or long grain rice
500 ml / 16 fl oz / 2 cups water
2 teaspoons salt
2.5 cm / 1 in cinnamon stick
3 small light-coloured cardamom pods, bruised
2 cloves
3 drops rose essence
2½ tablespoons melted ghee
3 tablespoons pouring cream
¼ teaspoon saffron strands, steeped for 15 minutes in 1 tablespoon hot milk

FOR THE GARNISH
1 tablespoon ghee
1 tablespoon slivered almonds
1 tablespoon unsalted pistachio nuts
1 tablespoon unsalted cashew nuts
rose petals
varak (silver leaf)

FOR THE CHICKEN

Blend the onions, ginger, garlic, almonds, poppy seeds and water to a smooth paste in a food processor. Set aside.

Heat the ghee in a heavy bottomed saucepan. Add the fennel seeds, cinnamon, and cloves, and fry for a few seconds to release their aromas. Add the blended paste and stir-fry over a medium heat for about 4 minutes, when the oil should start to separate out. Stir in the cardamom, cumin, coriander, chilli, nutmeg, mace and garam masala. If the mixture is inclined to stick, add a little water and keep stirring.

Add the chicken pieces, salt and raisins; stir to coat the chicken pieces. Cover and simmer gently for 15 minutes, stirring occasionally. Stir in the yogurt, and simmer until the moisture is absorbed. Sprinkle with the saffron threads and milk. Discard the cinnamon stick and set aside for 30 minutes to dry. Pre-heat the oven to 160 C / 325 F / Gas Mark 3.

Wild boar hunt in southern Rajasthan, *c.* 1775. A close connection between the Muslim court and its Hindu Rajput allies is evident from the Mughal court style of the men's dress.

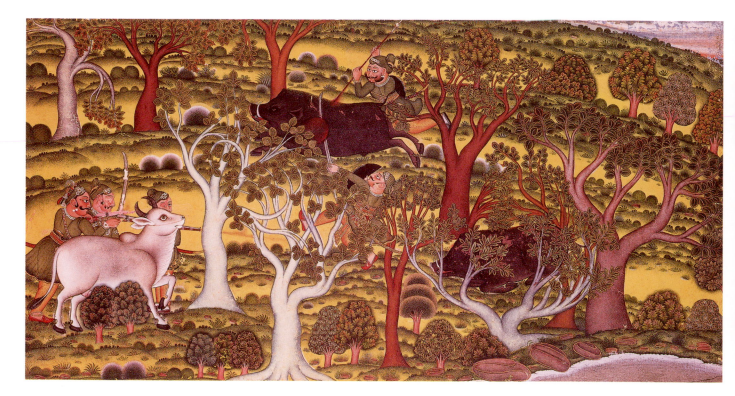

FOR THE RICE

Rinse the rice until the water runs clear. Cover it with water and soak for 30 minutes, then drain and set aside for 30 minutes to dry. Put the drained rice in a heavy bottomed saucepan with the water, cinnamon, cardamom, cloves and rose essence. Bring to the boil on a high heat. Cover with a close-fitting lid, reduce to a low heat, and simmer for 8 minutes. The rice will not be quite cooked, but most of the liquid will be absorbed. Fork through gently and discard the cinnamon stick and cardomom pods.

Grease a heavy bottomed oven-proof casserole with about half a tablespoon of the melted ghee. Arrange alternate even layers of rice and the chicken mixture. The number of layers will depend on the size of the casserole but I have assumed 2 layers. Start with a layer of rice, then evenly distributed chicken pieces; dribble each layer with cream and melted ghee, and sprinkle with saffron threads in milk. Repeat for as many layers as the dish will accommodate. Cover with a close-fitting lid and crimp foil around the edge to seal and trap the steam.

Bake in the pre-heated oven for 20 minutes. Fork through and gently mound onto a serving platter.

FOR THE GARNISH

Heat the ghee in a frying pan and toss and fry the nuts to a golden colour. Surround the edge of the rice with rose petals and sprinkle the mixed nuts over the surface. Flutter a few sheets of edible silver over the rice.

Saag Moghlai

SERVES 8

This dish is very quick and easy to make and is best if cooked just before serving.

6 tablespoons ghee
12 green cardamom pods
1 level teaspoon cumin seeds
1 level teaspoon fennel seeds

4 shallots, grated
1 tablespoon fresh ginger, grated
150 g / 6 oz field mushrooms, chopped roughly
600 g / 1 lb 6 oz fresh spinach, washed and well-dried
6 tablespoons double cream
juice 1½ lemons
1 level teaspoon salt
3 tablespoons flaked (sliced) almonds

Heat the ghee in a heavy bottomed pan and when it is hot, but not smoking, add the cardamom pods, cumin, and fennel seeds. Fry them all together for a minute, then add the grated shallots and grated ginger and fry for a further 2 minutes, stirring well and making sure they do not burn. Add the mushrooms and continue to fry for a further 3–4 minutes or until they start to give their juice. Finally add the spinach, cover the pan and wilt for 3–4 minutes. You will need to uncover the pan and stir the spinach quite regularly to make sure that it all gets cooked. Add the cream, lemon juice and salt, and mix well.

Turn onto a serving dish and sprinkle with the white flaked (sliced) almonds.

Khichri

SERVES 8

The combination of rice and dal or pulses was popular from the soldiers' mess to the emperor's table. It was a favourite of Akbar, perhaps recalling his campaigning days. It is sustaining, easy to heat, and travels well. This version is slightly more exotic. Make it a day in advance and the flavours will get a chance to develop.

100 g / 4 oz mung dal (mung beans), well rinsed
100 g / 4 oz basmati rice, well rinsed
25 g / 1 oz piece of fresh ginger, peeled and sliced into thin rounds
1½ litres / 2½ pints / 3¾ cups water
1½ teaspoons salt

A man of royal or noble descent sits on a throne in a garden, and is offered
refreshments and entertainment. Painting by Dharmdas, 1595.

This drawing of four men having refreshments under a tree is by Rembrandt, and was inspired by 17th-century Mughal miniature paintings.

freshly ground black pepper
4 tablespoons ghee
2 onions, chopped roughly
1 tablespoon finely chopped garlic
2 teaspoons cumin powder
1½ teaspoons coriander powder

Put the dal, rice and ginger in a large pan. Add 1¼ litres / 2 pints / 5 cups of water and bring to the boil. Stir once, then cover and simmer gently for about 1½ hours or until you have a porridge-like consistency. During the last 40 minutes, stir every 10 minutes or so to stop it sticking to the bottom of the pot. If it becomes too thick add a little extra water. When it has finished, remove the ginger, and add the salt and plenty of black pepper. Stir well.

Meanwhile, heat the ghee in a heavy pan and add the onions and garlic. Cook gently until all the moisture has evaporated from the onions, then add the cumin and coriander powders. Continue to fry over a medium heat for a further 6–8 minutes or until the onions colour. Pour the mixture over the khichri and cover immediately. After a minute, uncover and stir well to amalgamate the flavours.

Kulfi

serves 8

After such a feast you would be quite in order only to serve fresh fruit for dessert. The Mughals were great lovers and growers of fruits. One of the happiest entries in Babur's diaries records the arrival in Agra of some of the first grapes and melons from the stock that he had imported from Kabul and planted in Hindustan. However, if you wish for something a little more exotic, the classic Indian Kulfi would be ideal.

1.2 litres / 2 pints / 5 cups whole milk
8 green cardamom pods
2 tablespoons sugar
25 g / 1 oz ground (powdered) almonds
25 g / 1 oz finely chopped pistachios
1 tablespoon rosewater

Put the milk in a heavy saucepan and bring slowly to the boil. Add the cardamon pods, reduce to a simmer and continue to cook gently until the milk is reduced to 600 ml / 1 pint – this may take a couple of hours.

Remove the cardamom pods and stir in the sugar, ground almonds, half the pistachio nuts and the rosewater. Continue to stir as the mixture cools, and when it is quite cold pour into 6 dariole moulds or ramekin dishes and freeze.

Remove from freezer to refrigerator 30 minutes before you need to serve to allow the kulfi to soften. Unmould onto a single serving dish or individual dishes, and sprinkle with the remaining chopped pistachios.

6

The Cuisine of the Aztecs

A Franciscan monk seems an unlikely champion of the Aztec language and way of life, but without Fray Bernardino de Sahagun we would know little of the civilization that Hernando Cortez conquered in 1520. Born around 1500 at Sahagun in the Kingdom of Leon, Fray Bernardino took his vows as a Franciscan monk at the convent of Salamanca. A formidable scholar, he had a fine ear for language and an objectivity rare for his age and his profession. In 1529 he was sent to the college of Santa Cruz near Tenochtitlan (Mexico City) to instruct the native youth in Spanish, Latin, science, music and religion. He rapidly mastered Nahuatl, the Aztec language, and his superiors instructed him to compile, in Nahuatl, a compendium of all things relating to native history and custom which might be useful in 'Christianizing' the natives. He was given access to a dozen elders to instruct him: 'With these appointed principal men I talked many days during about two years, following the order of the minutes [the plan for the eventual Codex] which I had already made out. On all the subjects on which we conferred they gave me pictures – which were the writings anciently in use among them – and these grammarians interpreted to me their language'.

The twelve-volume manuscript was not finished until 1569 (Bernadino's Franciscan vow of poverty meant

OPPOSITE Tlaloc, the Aztec god of fertility, rain and agriculture, is depicted here with a maize plant and a pitcher of beans. From Codex Maglia-bechiano facsimile.

RIGHT Pottery plate with deer glyph, 1200–1521. The Aztecs loved the beautiful polychrome ceramics from Cholula, and Aztec iconography sometimes featured in the designs. From Cholula, Mexico.

Page from the Codex Tepetlaoztoc, c. 1555 (f.214v), so called after the town and showing the annual tribute exacted by the Spaniards, which included food such as beans, flour and chickens as well as gold and precious jewels.

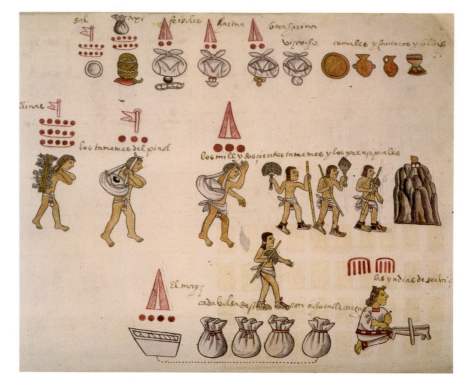

that he was denied clerical assistance). The President of the Council of the Indies in Spain asked Bernardino to make a complete Spanish translation, but this was not published, partly because the Spanish authorities feared that it might encourage educated natives to dwell upon their 'heathen' past, but mainly because they disapproved of his strictures on the methods of the Conquistadores. The translation was re-discovered in the early 1800s when it was published in three volumes in Mexico in 1829, and as part of *Kingsborough's Mexican Antiquities* in London in 1831.

The Florentine Codex, as it came to be known, covered every aspect of Aztec life – including their agriculture, their markets, their cooking utensils and, in great detail, their food. Although Fray Bernardino's information is said to have come from his informers, it is hard to believe that he did not wander the great market of Tenochtitlan himself, watching the tortilla makers, the chilli sellers, the breeders of hairless dogs, the makers of sauces and tamales, and the sellers of fine chocolate. The heart of the Aztec empire, Tenochtitlan was a bustling city of

250,000 people at the southwestern end of Lake Texoco. To feed such a large population every centimetre of land was farmed or cultivated in some way. Water channels or canals were dug out through the marshes, and the mud from these channels was used with small bushes and plants to make *chinampas* (rectangular platforms of land which could be anything from 30 to 1000 square meters in size). Here farmers lived and cultivated maize, beans, vegetables and herbs; bred turkeys, ducks and dogs; and fished for lake fish and insects. Daily they set off in boats with their wares for the great market, which was said to have attracted at least 25,000 people each day.

Maize and the products made from it were not only the staple food of the Aztecs, consumed in some guise for every meal, but also played a major part in Aztec religion, although Fray Bernardino only describes eight varieties – the yellow maize, the reddish, the tawny, the flower maize, the blue husked, the black maize, the black flyspecked maize with large soft, thick kernels speckled with black, and the white maize ear. The maize was softened in wood ashes and lime, then ground to make tortillas which, in their infinite variety, formed the basis of every meal for rich and poor alike. Fray Bernardino describes tortillas being sold in the market: 'The food seller sells tortillas which are thick, thickish, thick overall, extremely thick; he sells thin ones, thin tortillas, stretched out tortillas; dislike, straight with shelled beans … tortillas with meat and grains of maize, folded with chile, ashen tortillas, washed tortillas. He sells folded tortillas… tortillas with turkey eggs, made with honey, pressed ones, glove shaped tortillas, plain tortillas, squash tortillas…'

The other major maize-based food was 'tamales' – maize dough wrapped around meat, beans, chillis or fish, then wrapped in corn husks and steamed. Tamales came in as many varieties as tortillas. Once again Fray Bernardino lists those available in the market: 'meat tamales, plain tamales, tamales cooked in an earth oven … tamales with chile, fish tamales, frog tamales, tadpoles with grains of maize, mushrooms with grains of maize… narrow tamales, wide tamales, pointed tamales, spotted tamales … white fruit tamales, red fruit tamales, brick tamales…' Both the tortillas and the tamales were served (and sold) with sauces, most of which were based on combinations of chilli and tomatoes: 'He sells hot sauces, sauces of juices, with squash seeds, with tomatoes, with smoked chile, with hot chile, with mild red chile sauce, yellow chile sauce; bean sauce; toasted beans, mushrooms sauce, sauce of small squash, sauce of large tomatoes, sauce of ordinary tomatoes, sauce of avocados ...' They were also served with 'casseroles', which included chillis, tomatoes, fish, 'frogs and green chile, grey brown fish with red chile and ground squash seeds...' Fray Bernadino concludes, '...casseroles of large winged ants and locusts – very tasty food'. The meats included any of the huge range of wild fowl and game which roamed the mountains around the Valley of Mexico, as well as domesticated animals such as turkeys, muscovy ducks and edible dogs. Turkeys were much smaller and more compact than a modern over-bred bird, and were raised in massive quantities (one of the suburban markets around Tenochtitlan was said to sell 8,000 birds every five days). Dog breeding for food was also a lucrative profession. Probably fed on a diet of maize, dogs were much sought after.

It is unlikely that much sea fish reached Tenochtitlan as transport through the Aztec empire was very slow, but Lake Texoco itself provided a varied diet for its inhabitants – Fray Bernardino mentions many-coloured fish, as well as algae and large insects, with their eggs, which infested the lake and which made 'good, abundant and not disagreeable food'. Beans were the other staple of the daily diet. Fray Bernardino describes twelve different varieties, including the yellow bean with its well-known attendant problem: 'It can be stewed, it can be parched. It is fragrant, savoury, pleasing, very pleasing; it is edible in moderation. It causes flatulence in one – it distends the stomach. Grains of maize can be added'. In fact this combination of beans with maize was very popular, and provides an almost totally balanced diet. Apart from the ubiquitous chillis and tomatoes, squash (pumpkin) was also widely used. The seeds were very popular in sauces, casseroles and tamales. Mushrooms and avocados have already been mentioned in the context of sauces, but the Aztecs also used many leaves and herbs, both fresh and as seasonings, in those same sauces and casseroles.

The Aztecs were also great fruit eaters and although sweet dishes were known – sweetened with honey or agave syrup – most meals ended with fresh fruit and, for the lords at least, a drink of chocolate. Cacao beans did not grow in the Valley of Mexico and had to be imported from the south. The beans were valued not only as a food but as a coinage – for example it took 180 cacao beans to buy a small mantle or cloak, or a canoe-load of fresh water if you lived on the salty part of the lake. The beans were fermented, cured and toasted, then ground on the *metate* (grinding stone). Tepid water was added and a 'head' created by pouring the chocolate from one dish to another. Maize and innumerable flavourings such as vanilla, chilli and aromatic flowers could be added, along with honey and seeds of the piztle which would give the flavour of bitter almonds. The mixture could then be beaten or poured again to improve the head and be served tepid.

Finally, alcohol should be mentioned, albeit briefly. The Aztecs very much disapproved of drunkenness, so although alcohol could be fermented from a wide range of plants its consumption was not encouraged – except in old age. The sap from the maguey plant, a species of agave, was fermented in a drink called 'pulque' and this was permitted for old men and women over seventy who had grandchildren, as it was thought that their blood had turned cold and they needed the stimulation. Even then pulque drinking was regarded as plebeian, as lords, princes and warriors rarely consumed it, preferring to stick to chocolate.

Making tortillas is acknowledged to be no mean art. Ready-made tortillas are fairly easily available, so I have not suggested that you should try to make them. Aztec tortillas would have been made from corn, whereas many of the ready-made twenty-first century tortillas are made from wheat flour. In modern Mexico tortillas are usually filled, then heated in the oven and covered with sauce. Aztec tortillas were used, as are flat breads in the Middle East and India, as a means of conveying the food to your mouth so would be eaten in the hand and dipped in the sauce. Feel free to serve them as you feel inclined.

In pre-Columbian Mexico, as in Mexico today, you could buy an almost infinite variety of both chillis and tomatoes. I have suggested combinations of large beefy type tomatoes with lots of liquid-bearing flesh, and small sweet cherry or plum tomatoes with far greater skin areas and more concentrated flavours. If you can find a wider variety, feel free to experiment with any of the

Detail of a male porter with tribute demanded by the Spaniards. Codex Tepetlaoztoc, f.214v, *c.* 1555.

suggestions below. I have also used a combination of fresh, dried, mild and very hot chillis. Take care with the very hot varieties as a little goes a very long way. If you cannot get fresh chillis, you can use dried ones in all the recipes (soak them in hot to boiling water for 10–15 minutes before you use them). As always when dealing with chillis, treat them with great circumspection. If you are using the very hot varieties such as Hot Bonnet you may want to use rubber gloves. In any case, do not touch your face or eyes with your fingers until you have washed your hands very thoroughly.

Tortillas

Allow at least 1 large or 2 small tortillas per person. They can be briefly heated in a microwave or filled, covered and heated in an oven or microwave. Serve with the bean or guinea fowl dishes below, with any of the sauces. The recipes are to feed 8, and you should have enough of the sauces for the tamales as well as the tortillas.

Stone sculpture of Chalchiuhtlicue, the Aztec water goddess. She was associated with spring water, rivers and lakes, and also with birth.

HOT CHILLI & TOMATO SAUCE

½ small Hot Bonnet or other really hot chilli, de-seeded and chopped very small
500 g / 1 lb 2 oz large round tomatoes, chopped roughly
250 g / 9 oz small plum of cherry tomatoes, chopped roughly
approx. 1 teaspoon sea or rock salt

Dry fry or 'roast' the chilli in a wide pan for a couple of minutes over a moderate heat. The chilli should crinkle up and fizz slightly but do not let it burn as that will make it taste bitter. Be careful not to stand right over it as the vapours can make you cough and catch your breath. Add the tomatoes and a scant teaspoon of salt. Bring back to the boil, then simmer, uncovered, for approximately an hour. Taste and add extra salt if needed. If you prefer a less hot sauce, substitute 2 fresh green chillies for the Hot Bonnet chilli.

PINTO BEAN SAUCE

The flavour of the beans will mature if you can cook them 12–24 hours in advance.

½ a fresh red chilli, de-seeded and chopped
½ a fresh green Hot Bonnet chilli, de-seeded and chopped
500 g / 1 lb 2 oz cooked pinto beans (you can used tinned beans, drained)
200 g / 7 oz large round or beef tomatoes, chopped roughly
300 g / 10 oz plum or cherry tomatoes
sea or rock salt

Dry fry or roast the chillis as above. Add the beans and the tomatoes, bring to the boil and simmer for 20–30 minutes until the tomatoes are quite broken down. Season to taste with salt if it needs it.

MUSHROOM SAUCE

1 large dried ancho chilli
250 g / 10 oz field mushrooms, roughly chopped in a food processor
250 g / 10 oz cherry or plum tomatoes, roughly chopped
2 tablespoons water
sea salt to taste

Dry fry or roast the chilli but take care not to burn it or it will become bitter. Soak the chilli for 10–15 minutes in hot water then remove, de-seed and chop fairly small. Return the chilli to the pan and add the mushrooms, the tomatoes and water. Bring to the boil and simmer, uncovered, for 45 minutes. Season to taste with salt.

AVOCADO SAUCE

2 large fresh avocados, peeled and pitted
½ green Hot Bonnet chilli, de-seeded and finely chopped
½ fresh mild green chilli, de-seeded and chopped quite small
2 tablespoons of pumpkin seeds
½ teaspoon sea or rock salt

In a moderate oven or under a grill roast or toast the pumpkin seeds until they are just colouring but do not burn. Process them lightly so that they are roughly chopped. Purée the avocados in a food processor then add the chillis and purée briefly again. Remove from the processor and stir in the pumpkin seeds and salt to taste. Cover tightly until you need it so that it does not lose its colour.

'Wild Turkeys'

I did not think that any readers would really want to experiment with dog meat so I have chosen to use fowl for this casserole. Since 21st-century turkeys bear little resemblance to Aztec turkeys, I have suggested guinea fowl as the nearest fairly easily obtainable alternative. Fray Bernardino talks about both roast and casseroled birds so I suggest that you use 2 guinea fowl, and roast one and casserole the other. Each bird will serve 4 people.

CASSEROLED GUINEA FOWL

1 dried ancho chilli
680 g / 1½ lb plum cherry tomatoes, chopped roughly
3 tablespoons pumpkin seeds
1 large guinea fowl
sea or rock salt

Dry fry or roast the chilli for a few minutes in a pan, but take care not to burn it or it will be bitter. Soak for 10 minutes in hot to boiling water then de-seed and chop quite small. Roast and chop the pumpkin seeds as above.

In a heavy casserole large enough to take the bird mix the chilli, tomatoes and pumpkin seeds. Cook together for 10–15 minutes or until the tomatoes have started to break down. Place the guinea fowl on top and sprinkle quite generously with salt. Bring to the boil, cover and reduce the heat so that the pot is just simmering. Continue to simmer for 2 hours. The dish can be cooked in advance and then gently re-heated when you are ready to eat it.

ROAST GUINEA FOWL

1 large yellow or red Hot Bonnet chilli

1 large guinea fowl

1 teaspoon oil or butter

2 tablespoons roasted and lightly processed pumpkin seeds

Heat the oven to 180 C / 350 F / Gas Mark 4. Halve and de-seed the chilli and put it inside the guinea fowl. Rub the outside of the bird with the oil or butter and cover with the pumpkin seeds. Roast uncovered for 1½ hours then serve with the other guinea fowl.

Tamales
Makes 8 fairly substantial tamales

The corn needed to make tamale dough, 'masa harina', is not easy to find. If you can locate either some ready-made tamale dough or indeed masa harina, follow the instructions on the pack to make your dough. I was unable to find either but I did find some white polenta 'flour' which actually made excellent tamales. If you cannot find white, you could use the yellow variety. Ideally the tamales should be wrapped in either corn husks or maguey leaves. If you cannot locate either you can use aluminium foil quite successfully.

2 small red Hot bonnet chillis, de-seeded and chopped small
500 g / 1 lb 2 oz cooked or tinned (and drained) red kidney beans
600 g / 1 lb 5 oz large red tomatoes, roughly chopped
200 g / 7 oz small plum or cherry tomatoes, roughly chopped
300 g / 11 oz cooked chicken or turkey meat, chopped small
salt if needed
600 g / 1 lb 5 oz coarse white or yellow maize or polenta
1600 ml / 3½ pints / 6¼ cups well-flavoured chicken or turkey stock

Dry fry or roast the chillis in a pan for a few minutes taking care not to burn. Add the beans and tomatoes, bring to the boil and simmer for 20 minutes. Add the chicken meat and continue to cook for a further 10–15 minutes. Season to taste with salt.

Meanwhile, put the maize or polenta into a large pan. Heat the stock and stir it gradually into the maize. Bring gently to the boil and simmer for 20–30 minutes or until the liquid is all absorbed and the maize fairly soft.

Tear off 8 largish pieces of aluminium foil or open out your corn husks or maguey leaves. Divide the maize into 8 portions and press out each into an oval shape on a piece of foil. Divide the filling into 8 portions and place a portion in the middle of each tamale. Using the foil or husks, fold over the tamale and roll it into a tight roll, turning over either end. Carefully place the 8 rolls in a large steamer pan over some hot water. Cover the pan tightly and steam briskly for 45 minutes to 1 hour.

Carefully unroll each tamale onto a dish and serve with any of the sauces above.

Fresh Fruit

Although the Aztecs grew and harvested many fruits, the majority of them are only to be found in Central and South America. One of the exceptions is pineapple, and slices of fresh pineapple make a perfect dessert after what could be a rather substantial meal.

Chocolate

Aztec chocolate goblet.

Unless you grind your own cacao beans, it would be impossible to taste chocolate quite as the Aztecs would have done, but the following recipe, based on one given by Sara Jayne Stanes in her excellent book, *Chocolate: the Definite Guide*, gives some idea. This will make enough for 8 small cups.

40 g / 1½ oz coarse maize flour
250 ml / 8 fl oz / 1 cup hot water
1 tablespoon honey
1 split vanilla pod, seeds scraped
250 ml / 20 fl oz / 2½ cups cold water
100 g / 4 oz Mexican chocolate (65–70% cocoa solids)

Mix the maize with the hot water and leave to stand for 15 minutes. Pour/spoon into a saucepan with the rest of the water, the honey, and vanilla pod. Cook over a medium heat, stirring for 10 minutes. Add the chocolate. Simmer for another 15 minutes, stirring regularly, until the chocolate melts. Remove the vanilla.

According to Fray Bernardino, pouring the chocolate from a height from pot to pot and into the cups should raise a froth. If you are failing to achieve this, a quick whiz with a mixer may help. The chocolate should be drunk tepid.

7

Dinner with Queen Elizabeth I

I n number of dishes and change of meat the nobilitie of England (whose cookes are for the most part musicall headed Frenchmen) doo most exceed, so that for a man to dine with them and to taste of every dish that standeth before him is rather to yield to a conspiracie with a great deal of meate for the speedie suppression of naturall health.

William Harrison wrote this about the English nobility in the 1580s, and so you would expect that the queen's tables would be even more liberally supplied. Indeed they were – but the queen did not partake. Despite her love of clothes and jewels, and unlike her father King Henry VIII, Queen Elizabeth I had little interest in food. She was an early riser and a keen walker, and her most substantial meal of the day, after a brisk walk, was her breakfast of 'beef and small beer'. What other meals she had (mainly cold meats and salads), she took alone. On Sundays Elizabeth was served with full formality in the great hall of wherever she might be residing, but having been served she would retire to her own rooms to eat. The only exception to this was when the weather was good enough for outdoor eating, as Elizabeth could not resist a picnic. The gardens of all the royal palaces were kept well stocked with scented flowers, and in the summer temporary 'banqueting houses' might be built in the garden.

LEFT Drawing of Queen Elizabeth I by Nicholas Hilliard, *c.* 1584.

OPPOSITE *Sir Henry Unton* by unknown artist, *c.* 1596. This detail shows a banquet in progress, with musicians playing in the foreground.

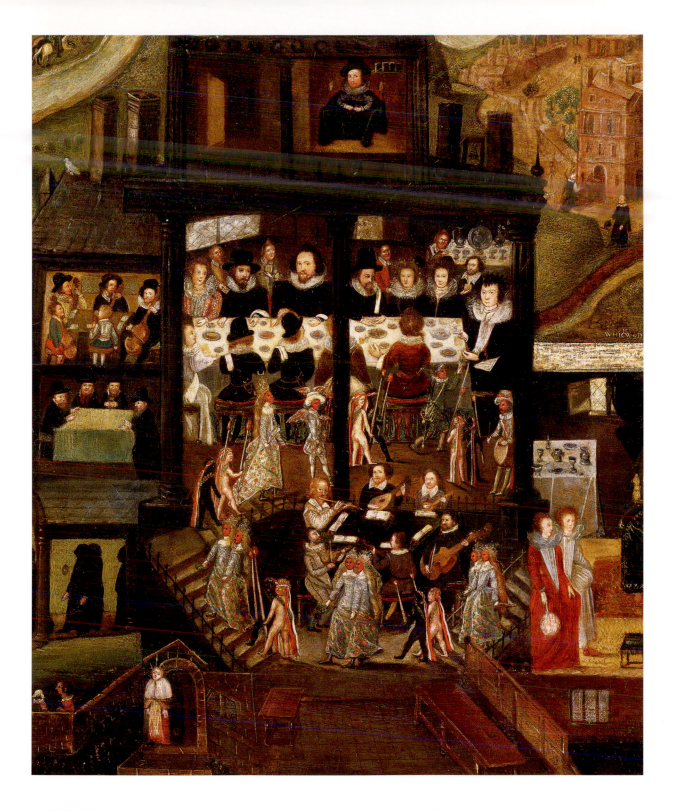

Queen Elizabeth I in a procession. From a 16th-century manuscript dedicated to Elizabeth I.

As a result of her temperance, royal official Sir Roger Wilbraham was able to write that the 'Queene was sound in her helth till her last sickness, strong of constitution, her only physician was her own observation and a good diett; not tied to hours of eating or sleeping but following appetite; not delighting in bellie cheere to please the taste but feeding always upon meates that susteyne and strenghten nature'. Her only weakness was for sweets and 'comfits', of which she received prodigious quantities as gifts, especially at New Year. It was her passion for sweets which rotted her teeth – a defect on which several sixteenth-century travellers commented, although the offending teeth never appeared in her portraits.

But if the queen ate sparingly, the same could not be said for the rest of her court. Tudor monarchs moved continually around the country, staying both in royal residences and as guests of the great lords. In the days of poor communication (roads were still little more than cart tracks and twenty miles was a very substantial day's travel), this was a good way to remind one's subjects of one's presence. The accompanying court could consist of more than five hundred people, including servants and visitors, and few areas were fertile enough to supply that number of extra mouths for more than a few weeks. Indeed, so expensive could this operation be that the nobility did their best to escape royal visits. Poor Sir John Cutte, who had been Henry VIII's treasurer, was visited twice at Horham Hall, the second visit in 1578 putting him into the bankruptcy court.

Elizabethan feasts allowed for this peripatetic way of life. As in the Middle Ages, trestle tables were set up in the great hall, rushes strewed on the ground, and the walls covered with hangings and tapestries which helped to keep out the draughts but were easy to take down and transport. Although Elizabeth's reign saw a huge increase in the amount of glass used in windows, halls were still dark and gloomy, so displays of silver, gold and pewter plate helped to reflect the light of rush and tallow candles. For the rich, 'plates' were made from gold, silver or pewter; for the middle men they were of wood, while poorer guests would eat from trenchers (slabs of stale bread). The rich would eat with gold and silver knives and spoons; forks only came into use at the end of the century, possibly to help get your food to your mouth without soiling the huge ruff around your neck. The lesser folk ate with horn or wooden spoons and their fingers.

Engraved glass goblet. England, 1586.

'Small' beer or ale (a good deal less powerful than modern beer and made without hops) was the common drink, with wines from France and Portugal for the gentry — all of which the queen, when she drank them at all, drank well watered.

The English were famous for the quantity and quality of the meat they consumed, much to the disgust of Philip Stubbes, author of *The Anatomie of Abuses* (1583): 'Nowadays, if the table be not covered from one end to the other, as thick as one dish can stand by another, with delicate meats of sundry sorts, one cleane different from another and to every dish severall sawces appropriate to his kind, it is thought unworthy the name of dinner'. Roast birds of all sizes from swans to mallards, roast meats from whole sides to individual dishes, various fish, dishes of soup and dishes of greens would grace any table. The meal was usually served in one, two or three courses to allow for entertainments during the meal — Elizabethans were nothing if not rowdy, and a court favourite was to have the jester dive headfirst into a large bowl of custard. Sweetmeats, candied flowers, marchpaynes (marzipans), gingerbreads, preserves and jellies would come at the end of the meal, and might well be served outside in a specially built banqueting hall.

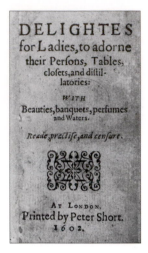

Frontispiece to
Sir Hugh Plat's
Delightes for Ladies,
first published in
1600.

The recipes I have chosen come from two of the few Elizabethan cookery writers whom we know something about. The first is Sir Hugh Plat, who was a gentleman, an inventor, a scientist and a tireless experimenter. His *Delightes for Ladies* gives relatively few instructions for actual dishes, preferring to provide endless recipes for distillations, preserves, perfume and face creams, and includes 'dentifrices or Rubbers for the teeth', 'a ball to take the staines from linnen' and 'how to keep flesh sweet in the summer'. We must assume, however, that the second, Thomas Dawson, was a professional cook. As part of the frontispiece of his *The Good Huswifes Jewel* (1596), he says, 'Wherein is to be found most excellent and rare Devices for conceites in Cookery, found out by the practice of Thomas Dawson'. He then lists various menus which include:

THE FIRST COURSE FOR SUPPER
*A Salet, A Pigges petitoe, powdered Beefe, a Shulder of Mutton
or a Breaste, Veale, Lambe, custard.*

THE SECOND COURSE
*Capons Rosted, Connies (rabbits) Rosted, Chickens rosted, Pigeons
rosted, Larkes Rosted, A Pye of pygeons or chickins, Baked Venison, Tart.*

SERVICE FOR FISHE DAIES
*Butter, a Sallet with Hard Egges, potage (soup), Red herring, White herring,
Lyng, Mustard, Salte Salmon minc'd. Two pasties and a Custard.*

SECOND COURSE
*Flounders with Pyke sauce, Fresh salmon, Fresh Conger (eel), Turbot, Halybut,
sauce Vineger. Breame upon soppes, Carpe upon Soppes, Soles Fryed,
Roasted Lamperns, Rosted porpos, fresh Sturgeon,
sauce Galentine. Shrimps sauce Vineger.
Figges, Apples, almoundes blanched, Cheese, Raysins, Peares.*

With your Elizabethan feast you can drink ale (not beer), or French wines which had been popular amongst the gentry since the Middle Ages when English kings ruled over substantial portions of the wine-growing regions of France.

To Make a Cullis as White as Snow
(Sir Hugh Plat)

SERVES 8

Still-Life with Oysters and Pastries by Osias Beert, 1610.

A cullis was a very rich stock, derived from large quantities of meat boiled over a long period to extract all the goodness.

1 small boiling chicken
100 g / 4 oz leeks, finely chopped
600 ml / 1 pint / 2½ cups white wine

900 ml / 1½ pints / 3¾ cups water
juice 1 lemon
bouquet garni
2 heaped teaspoons ground ginger
1 level teaspoon icing (superfine) sugar
300 ml / 10 fl oz single (regular) cream
sea salt and white pepper

Put the chicken (whole) in a deep pan with the leeks, wine, water, lemon juice and bouquet garni. Bring to the boil and simmer gently for 1½ hours.

Remove the chicken from the pot, strain the broth, allow it to cool, then chill it. According to Sir Hugh's recipe you should now dispose of the chicken flesh and use only the broth. If you don't wish to throw it out, cut it into thin slivers and preserve. When the broth has cooled entirely, remove any fat which has solidified on top. Return to a pan and re-heat.

Make a paste with the ginger, the sugar and a little cream. Add a little broth to make a smooth thin paste, then add it to the broth. Add the rest of the cream and re-heat gently. Season to taste with sea salt and white pepper before serving.

To Make Fritters of Spinnedge
(Thomas Dawson)

SERVES 8

Thomas Dawson's recipe requires coating the fritters in batter and deep frying them, which makes this a rather time consuming dish. I have adapted it slightly to make what was known as a froise (omelette), which can be served as part of your feast but which is also great as a dish on its own. It is tastes as good cold as hot, so it can be made in advance, and happily eaten the following day as a snack. If you do want to make fritters, however, directions are at the end of the recipe.

Tudor eggs were much smaller than ours so this froise needs nearer to 16 eggs to feed 8 people. If you want to make it a bit more substantial you could, as Elizabethans might have done, add some chopped cooked meat.

600 g / 1¼ lb fresh spinach — a mature, fairly coarse spinach if possible rather than young spinach leaves

100 g / 4 oz cooked beef, tongue, lamb, or chicken, chopped small (optional)

4 thick slices of stale wholemeal (wholewheat) bread, crumbed

3 level teaspoons each ground cinnamon and ground ginger

1 heaped teaspoon each light muscovado sugar and freshly ground black pepper

75 g / 3 oz currants

75 g / 3 oz dried dates, chopped very small

12 medium eggs

a knob of butter

Cook the spinach briskly in 25 cm / 1 in water for 5–6 minutes or until it is quite cooked. Drain very thoroughly and chop small. Mix the spinach in a large bowl with the chopped meat (if you are using it), the breadcrumbs, spices, sugar and dried fruit. Add the eggs and beat/mix thoroughly.

Heat the butter in a large wide pan until it sizzles. Pour in the mixture and cook steadily, not too fast, until the froise is quite solid below. Meanwhile heat a grill or broiler. Put the pan under the grill or broiler for another 3–4 minutes to cook the top of the froise. Slide the froise gently onto a serving dish and serve hot, or leave to cool and serve at room temperature.

To make fritters, double the amount of breadcrumbs in the mixture, then roll the mixture into soup-spoon size balls. Make a batter with 100 g / 4 oz whole-meal (wholewheat) flour, 1 egg and 240 ml / 8 fl oz / 1 cup beer. Beat thoroughly in a food processor. Heat oil in a deep fryer until just smoking. Using a slotted spoon or two forks, dip each of the balls into the batter and drop in the hot fat. Allow to fry briskly till lightly tanned all over, then drain on kitchen paper and keep warm. Continue until all the balls are cooked and serve at once.

To Make Stewed Steakes
(Thomas Dawson)

SERVES 8

Dawson's recipe works equally well with lamb or with beef. 'Soppes' were thick slices of bread which were designed to soak up the juices and then be eaten after the meat.

8 x 225 g / 8 oz lamb or beef steaks
400 ml / 14 fl oz / 1¼ cups ale or beer (use a fairly light beer)
400 ml / 14 fl oz / 1¼ cups rough red wine
2 sprigs each of fresh rosemary, thyme and parsley or 1 teaspoon of each dried
2 small onions, sliced into thin rounds
4 softened prunes, stoned and chopped small
4 softened, dried dates, stoned and chopped small
a handful each of raisins and currants
4 cloves
small piece of ginger root, peeled
½ stick cinnamon
½ teaspoon grated nutmeg
8 thick slices of fairly stale rough brown bread
Fresh or frozen redcurrants or raspberries to garnish

Put the steaks in a wide saucepan, add the wine and beer, and bring quickly to the boil. Skim off any scum which may rise to the surface. Reduce the temperature, and add the herbs and the onions. Cover the pot and simmer for 10 minutes. Add the dried fruits and spices and continue to simmer, covered, for a further 30 minutes. Remove the branches of rosemary and thyme if you were using fresh.

Lay the bread slices out on a dish or on individual plates, and lay one steak on each slice of bread. With a slotted spoon, divide the soft fruits and lay them on top of the steaks. Pour over the cooking juices and decorate with the redcurrants or raspberries.

To Roast Carpe or Tench with a Pudding in his Belly
(Thomas Dawson)

SERVES 8

Tench and carp are both river fish, but it is almost impossible to buy tench nowadays. However, carp can be got from a fishmonger, especially in Jewish areas as it is a traditional Jewish holiday dish. Carp are spectacular looking, but can taste quite muddy if they have not been living in a swift flowing river. If you do not want to use carp you could use the same recipe with a salmon or a small halibut.

You are unlikely to obtain pike bones (used in the 16th century to give texture), but if you wish to follow the spirit of the recipe you could use the bones from 2 x 120 g tins of sardines or from a cooked sole or plaice, well crushed in a food processor or with the back of a heavy knife.

Barberries are the very tart fruit of the shrub, *Berberis*. The best modern-day equivalent would be redcurrants, or cranberries if redcurrents are out of season.

1 x 2–3 kilo / 4–6 lb carp (or salmon or halibut), cleaned but with its head and tail
left on the bones from your fish, well crushed (see above)
half a small loaf of wholemeal (wholewheat) bread, grated into crumbs
2 eggs
25 g / 1 oz currants

> *Take the bones of a pike and choppe them very smalle, then put in grated bread, two or three egges, currans, dates, suger, cinnamon and Ginger, and Mace, Pepper and salte, and put it in his bellye, and put him on a Broche, and make sweete sauce with Barberyes, and Lemmons minced, and put into the sweete sauce, and then put it on the Carpe when you serve it up.*

Women gutting fish, by an unknown artist, 1598.

25 g / 1 oz soft dried dates, chopped very small

1 level teaspoon caster (superfine) sugar

1 level teaspoon each ground cinnamon and ginger

½ level teaspoon each mace and freshly ground black pepper

1 level teaspoon sea salt

50 g / 2 oz butter

100 g / 4 oz redcurrants or cranberries

1 lemon, cut up

1 tablespoon light muscovado sugar

120 ml / 4 fl oz / ½ cup sweet red wine such as Marsala

120 ml / 4 fl oz / ½ cup water

Heat the oven to 180 C / 350 F / Gas Mark 4. In a bowl thoroughly mix the bones of the fish (if you are using them), the breadcrumbs, eggs, dried fruits, sugar and seasoning. Use to stuff the belly of the fish. Butter a large baking dish all over, then lay the stuffed fish into it. Butter the top of the fish thoroughly, then cover with aluminium (baking) foil. Bake for 40 minutes per kilo (20 minutes per pound) of fish.

Meanwhile, pulverize the lemon and the cranberries, with the sugar, in a food processor. Turn the mixture into a small saucepan and add the sweet wine and the water. Cover and simmer gently for 20 minutes.

Carefully move the fish, whole, from the baking tray onto a warmed platter, to serve accompanied by a dish of the sauce.

To Make a Close Tarte of Cherries
(Thomas Dawson)

SERVES 8

Cherries were known to be one of Queen Elizabeth's favourite fruit – and even in the 16th century Kent was famous for its cherry orchards. A 'close' tart means a covered tart so when Thomas Dawson tells you to 'close them', he means to cover the cherries with a pastry lid.

The egg yolks in Thomas' recipe for Butter Paste make it very rich and rather heavy, so I have used a simpler butter crust. Since it was not possible to mill flour so as to crush the grain until the roller mills of the 19th century, even the finest of 16th-century wheat flour would still have been closer to our wholemeal (whole-wheat) flour.

1.5 kilos / 3 lbs 5 oz fresh cherries (if cherries are totally out of season you could use 1 kilo / 2 lb frozen or canned)
2 heaped teaspoons ground cinnamon
2 heaped teaspoons ground ginger
2 heaped teaspoons light muscovado sugar
5 tablespoons cherry brandy, Crème de Cassis, or other red fruit liqueur
6 tablespoons water
150 g / 6 oz wholemeal (wholewheat) flour
25 g / 1 oz light muscovado sugar
100 g / 4 oz butter
water to mix

Wash and stone the cherries if fresh. Defrost or drain if frozen or canned. Put the spices, sugar, liqueur and water in a small pan and bring it to the boil. Cover and cook at just below boiling point for 5 minutes. Turn the cherries into a pie dish and pour over the spice mixture.

Heat the oven to 190 C / 275 F / Gas Mark 5. Rub the butter into the flour and mix to a soft dough with cold water. Roll the pastry out on a floured board to slightly larger than the shape of the pie dish. Cut a narrow border of pastry to lay around the edge of the pie dish. Moisten the edge of the dish with a little water and lay on the border. Moisten the pastry edge and lay the pastry lid (rolling it up over the rolling pin) on top of the pie. Secure the edge by pressing it with a finger, blunt knife edge, or fork, and decorate with the remaining pastry scraps.

Bake for 25 minutes or until the pastry lid is crisp and just colouring. Remove from the oven and sprinkle with a little extra sugar. Serve warm or at room temperature.

Take out the stones and laye them as whole as you can in a Charger, and put Mustard and Synamon and ginger to them, and lay them in a Tarte whole, and close them, and let them stand thus quarter of an houre in the Oven, then take a sirrope of Muscadine, and damask water and sugar, and so serve it.

TO MAKE A BUTTER PASTE
Take floure and seven or eight egges and cold butter and faire water, or rosewater, and spices (as you will) and make your paste and beat it on a boorder, and when you have so done, devide it into two or three partes and drive out the piece with a rowling pinne, and doe with butter one piece by another, and then folde up your paste upon the butter and drive it out again, and so do five or sixe times together, then put them to the Oven and when they be baked, scrape suger on them and so serve them.

8

Jewish Passover Supper: Centuries of Tradition

The Tribes of Israel who were forced out of the Holy Land in the first millennium AD moved both north and south. Those who travelled south spread through northern Africa and up into Spain. They were the ancestors of the Sephardi Jews, and their food was greatly influenced by the local foods of the countries in which they settled. Those who moved north settled in Eastern Europe, Germany, Russia and the Baltic States, and became known as the Ashkenazi (*Ashkenaz* is the Hebrew word for Germany). The huge migrations of the nineteenth and early twentieth centuries to Western Europe and the USA were of these Ashkenazi Jews, taking with them the foods and traditions of north-eastern Europe.

The life of the Ashkenazi in early Christian Europe was difficult. They were shunned by the Christian population as 'Christ killers', and restricted in what work they could do. Whenever anything went wrong in the community, all too often they bore the blame and were forced to flee from Christian wrath and revenge. As a result Jewish communities were self-contained and inward-looking, held together by religious observance and by a common language, Yiddish. Although by the late Middle Ages there was a Jewish community in most towns (usually living in a specific settlement or ghetto),

LEFT Seder plate. Made in Karlsbad, *c.* 1880–1900.

OPPOSITE *The Feast of the Passover* by Dieric Bouts the Elder, 1464–7.

The master of the house supervises the distribution of Passover food such as unleavened bread and sweetmeats. From *The Golden Haggadah, c.* 1320.

the majority of the Jewish population lived in small rural communities or *shetls*. Due to the insecurity of their position within a Christian society, the only place that a Jew could really feel safe was within the home. The memory of constant hardship and frequent flight gave that home, and especially the kitchen, a position of prime importance in Jewish life. Food was a way of communicating love and security within the home, while the rituals surrounding its preparation cemented the community together.

The kitchen was the heart of every household. It was a place of constant family activity, warmth and good fellowship, where the Jewish matriarch reigned supreme. Although Jewish women were not required to perform all the daily religious rituals, they frequently bore the financial responsibility of feeding and clothing the family while the man of the house devoted himself to religious study. The women also educated the children, educating girls entirely and boys until they went to school at the age of three. Money was often earned by extending the work needed to feed the family — running a small grocery shop, cooking speciality goods or fattening geese and chickens. Because of the complexity of the dietary laws and the number of highly ritualized holidays, running a Jewish kitchen was extremely complicated. The esteem in which the Jewish woman was held depended on how creatively she managed her manifold tasks.

As well as the eight major Jewish festivals each year, all of which had complex rituals attached, there were the weekly requirements of the Shabbath plus the dietary restrictions (laws of Kashrut), which applied all year round. These laws forbade the consumption of animals unless they 'chewed the cud' and had cloven hooves, while only fish with both fins and scales could be eaten. More onerous were the laws that required the preparation, or 'koshering', of meat to avoid the consumption of blood, and which forbade the eating or cooking of milk and meat together. Both practices were interpreted as being forbidden by the scriptures. Strict observance of the milk/meat separation could mean effectively running two kitchens, one for meat and one for milk products.

Passover (or *Pesach*), the feast we are celebrating here, is one of the most important in the Jewish year and celebrates the Exodus of Moses and his followers from Egypt, which led to the birth of the Jewish race. There was not time to let their dough rise as they fled Egypt, and in memory of this no leaven is allowed in a Jewish house during the seven days of Passover. This prohibition includes any fermentation agent such as yeast, or any grain (or dish made from that grain)

Here, sheep are being slaughtered and skinned for Passover. From *The Golden Haggadah, c.* 1320.

which could ferment. Special meal (matzo meal), made from wheat which has been kept dry so cannot have fermented, is all that is allowed. Before the festival the house must also be entirely cleansed of any fermented foods. The ban on flour and yeast led to the development of dishes which relied on matzo meal, potato flour, and eggs as a raising and binding agent, and the wide use of nuts in baking and for desserts.

The most important events during Passover are the two Seder meals, which occur at the beginning of the festival. During the meal there are readings from the *Haggadah*, the book which tells the tale of the Exodus and which details how the meal should be served. A decorated plate or tray carries the following ritual foods:

Three *matzoth*
These are made from special bread to represent the three sections of ancient society.
Two are not eaten, but the third is shared among the company

Bitter herbs (*maror*) and young green leaves (*karpas*)
The herbs recall the bitterness of slavery, while the leaves represent new growth

Lemon juice or salt water (or sometimes vinegar) and
haroset, a fruit and nut paste
The juice or water represents the tears shed by the Jews in Egypt, and the *haroset* represents the
colour of the mortar used by the Jews when they were building pyramids for the Egyptians.
The herbs are dipped in these

A roasted shank bone of lamb
This represents the lamb sacrificed by the slaves on the eve of the Exodus.
It can also symbolize the strong hand of God delivering the Hebrews from Egypt

A roasted egg
This has many meanings attributed to it, including birth and re-birth, and recalls the
special festive offering brought to the Temple in Jerusalem in ancient times.
The egg is not eaten, but many families will serve hard-boiled eggs
with salt water at the beginning and end of the Seder meal.

There are no set dishes for the Seder meal, although all the dishes must conform not only to the laws of Kashrut but with the special Passover ban on leavening of any kind. I have therefore chosen the most classic Ashkenazi dishes, which would have been cooked throughout the Jewish communities of Russia, Germany and Eastern Europe for the last five hundred years.

Golden Yoich (or Chicken Soup with Knaidlach)

SERVES 10

No holiday meal would be complete without chicken soup, the most famous of all Jewish dishes for which there are as many recipes are there are Jewish families. The only two essential ingredients are the chicken and the parsley stalks. Ideally the broth should be made with a fat old boiling chicken, and gets it 'golden' name from the globules of golden fat floating on top – although these days the fat is normally skimmed off and the colour achieved with a pinch of saffron. 'Knaidl' is the Yiddish word for dumpling, and the Passover version, cooked with matzo meal, is so popular that it is cooked all year round. Knaidlach can include beef marrow, onions, parsley, almonds and chicken fat, and can be very substantial. Given the size of this Passover meal, I have chosen a light, fluffy recipe.

SOUP
1 large old boiling chicken, with giblets and feet if possible
4 litres / 6½ pints / 16 cups water
2 large onions, peeled and halved
2 large old carrots, scrubbed and chopped
2 turnips, scrubbed and sliced
2 sticks celery, scrubbed and chopped
4 mushrooms, wiped and halved
½ teaspoon saffron strands
3 bayleaves
a handful of fresh parsley with its stalks
1 teaspoon peppercorns

Put the chicken in a large pot with the water and bring very slowly to the boil. Skim any scum from the surface and simmer for 5 minutes, skimming any further

Hebrew script in the shape of a cockerel. From *The Ashkenazi Haggadah*, c. 1460–75.

scum which rises. Add the vegetables and herbs, bring back to simmer, cover and cook very gently for 1–1½ hours, depending on the age of the chicken.

Carefully remove the chicken from the pot and take most of the flesh off the bones (reserving it for another meal). Return the carcass to the pot, re-cover, and continue to cook gently for a further 2–3 hours.

Strain the broth through a fine sieve and discard the vegetables and carcass. Cover the broth, cool it and then chill it. Remove most of the fat from the top and reserve it for use in another dish. Reheat the broth, adjust the seasoning to taste, and serve with the knaidlach.

KNAIDLACH
Makes about 15 small dumplings

2 eggs, separated
75 g / 3 oz medium matzo meal
1 teaspoon salt
freshly ground black pepper

Separate the eggs. Beat the whites until quite stiff and beat the yolks lightly. Fold the yolks into the whites, followed by the matzo meal and the salt and pepper. You will need plenty to give them flavour. Chill for 30 minutes.

Bring a large pan of lightly salted water to the boil. Roll teaspoons of the mixture into small balls and drop them in the water. Reduce to a simmer and cook gently for 30 minutes. Remove and set aside on kitchen paper until you need them. (The knaidlach soak up a great deal of liquid, so it is not advisable to cook them in the soup.) To serve, re-heat the knaidlach in the boiling water, then drop them into the soup just before serving.

Gefilte Fish with Chrain

SERVES 10

Drawing of a
17th-century plate in
the Kunstgewerbe
Museum, Düsseldorf.

Like chicken soup, this stuffed fish dish is one for which every Jewish family has their own recipe. In medieval times it involved stuffing the skin of a carp or a pike with a chopped and seasoned mixture of fish. Nowadays the stuffing is normally poached and then served cold with the reduced and gellied stock in which it was cooked. Any combination of fish can be used, but there should always be more than one fish involved. In some countries, such as Poland, the fish is sweetened, while in others, such as Lithuania, it is peppery. The only other constant is that each fish ball should be topped by a slice of carrot. You should make the gefilte fish at least a day before you plan to serve them. Chrain is a delicious fresh beetroot and horseradish relish, whose colour and spiciness set off the gefilte fish to perfection.

GEFILTE FISH

Heads, skin and bones of several fish

4 onions, sliced finely

4 large carrots, scrubbed and cut crossways into very thin slices

4 sticks celery, cut into thin slices

1 kilo / 2 lb fresh fish — ideally a mixture of white sea fish (such as cod or haddock) with river fish (such as carp or pike), but if you cannot get the latter the sea fish alone is fine

2 eggs

2 tablespoons ground almonds

2 tablespoons medium matzo meal

2 heaped teaspoons salt

plenty of freshly ground black pepper

To make the stock, wash the heads and bones of the fish and put in a large pan with the vegetables, salt and pepper. Cover generously with cold water. Slowly bring to the boil, skim, then reduce the heat and simmer for 45 minutes. At this point you can remove the fish heads, bones and skin.

Traditionally the fish was chopped by hand, but it is much easier to use a food processor. Process the fish with half the onion, adding a little very cold water if the mixture seems too dry. Be careful not to process it into a paste. Spoon into a bowl and add the eggs, ground almonds, matzo meal, salt and pepper. Chill for at least 30 minutes.

To cook, re-heat the fish stock. Form the fish mixture into balls or patties about 4 cm / 1½ in across. Slide the balls into the stock and simmer, covered. Traditionally gefilte fish can be cooked for up to 1½ hours but this can make them rather tasteless. I cooked mine for 30 minutes, then turned off the heat and

A 19th-century Passover supper in New York. *Century Magazine*, January 1892.

allowed them to cool in the stock. When cold, remove the balls onto a serving dish and top each one with a slice of carrot.

Return the stock to the heat and continue to cook for a further hour, then cool and chill. Spoon the stock with the remaining carrots and the remaining onions, which should be at least partially jelled, around the fish balls.

CHRAIN

150 g / 6 oz fresh or bottled horseradish root, peeled and grated
350 g / 12 oz fresh raw beetroot, scrubbed, topped and tailed, and grated
120 ml / 4 fl oz / ½ cup wine vinegar

Mix all three ingredients together thoroughly and store in a tightly sealed jar in the fridge. It loses its fire if exposed to the air.

Roast Goose

SERVES 10

Since the Middle Ages geese have held an important place in the Jewish kitchen. The bird itself was traditional festive fare, while the fat was used for both cooking and waterproofing and the feathers were needed for bedding and pillows. The birds are very rich, very fat, and can be tough, so they need careful cooking and sharp accompaniments – such as the red cabbage and apple dish on page 103.

1 large goose with its giblets
5 small cooking apples or tart eating apples
10 small onions
3 tablespoons raisins
2 tablespoons ground almonds
2 tablespoons olive oil
liver of the goose, chopped small
225 g / 8 oz open mushrooms, chopped small

8 shallots, peeled and chopped finely
100 g / 4 oz roasted hazelnuts
100 g / 4 oz broken walnuts
handful of parsley, chopped
2 eggs
salt, pepper, and pinch of cinnamon

Core the cooking apples and peel the onions. Mix 2 tablespoons of raisins with the ground almonds. Stuff the mixture into the cooking apples. Fill the cavity of the goose with the apples and onions.

Heat the oil and lightly fry the goose liver with the mushrooms and shallots. Add the remaining raisins. Grind the nuts in a food processor until they are quite fine, taking care not to turn them into paste. Add to the goose liver and mushrooms. Mix well, remove from the heat and add the parsley, eggs and seasoning. Use this mixture to stuff the neck of the goose. Prick the goose all over, cover the breast with foil, and place the goose on a rack above a baking tray.

Bake the goose in a moderate oven (350 F / 170 C / Gas Mark 4) for 15 minutes to the pound, or in a slow oven for 25 minutes to the pound. About 45 minutes before the goose is done, remove the foil from the breast to allow it to brown.

Serve the sliced goose with an onion and half an apple for each person, and the red cabbage.

Red Cabbage with Apple

SERVES 10

Before the arrival of the potato, the only vegetables available to Ashkenazi cooks in northeastern Europe were cabbages and carrots. This combination of red cabbage with apple is also a popular north German dish, and is an excellent foil to the richness of the goose.

4 tablespoons olive oil
2 medium onions, peeled and chopped
1 bulb fennel, chopped small
1.25 kg / 2½ lb red cabbage, sliced fairly thinly
3 small cooking apples or tart eating apples, peeled, cored and chopped
2 teaspoons caraway seeds
4 tablespoons red wine vinegar
4 tablespoons sweet red wine, such as Marsala
salt and pepper
a bunch of fresh dill weed
optional — 10 tablespoons plain yogurt

Heat the oil in a large pan and add the onions and fennel. Cook gently for about 10 minutes or until the vegetables are starting to soften.

Add the cabbage, apples, seeds, vinegar and wine. Cover the pan tightly and cook gently for 15–20 minutes or until the cabbage is soft, but still has some crunch. Season to taste with salt and pepper.

Sprinkle with chopped dill weed before serving. If you wish to use the yogurt, put one tablespoon on the top of each serving on the plate.

Prune Tzimmes

SERVES 10

The word 'tzimmes' covers a wide range of slow-cooked, one-pot stews, usually containing meat, sweet vegetables and fruit, although they can be made without the meat. For most Jewish people the golden carrot tzimmes (cooked honeyed carrots) are the most familiar, but each country had its favourite combinations. In Germany prunes were always included; in Poland and Russia, carrots and fruits; in Romania, chickpeas and pumpkin. However, all tzimmes were generously seasoned with black pepper to counteract the sweetness of the fruit. In Yiddish the word means 'mixed together', but because the stews were usually made for a festival meal, it has also come to mean 'a big fuss'. Tzimmes can be served as a starter, a side dish, a main dish or even as a dessert. I have combined the German passion for prunes with the Romanian pumpkin.

2 kilo / 4 lb rolled brisket, flank, or rolled rib of beef
3 tablespoons chicken fat (schmaltz) or olive oil
3 medium onions, peeled and chopped roughly
a 1 kilo / 2lb piece of pumpkin, peeled, de-seeded and cut into large dice
750 g / 1 lb 10 oz pitted prunes
1 tablespoon honey
1 level teaspoon grated nutmeg
1 heaped teaspoon ground ginger
1 large wine glass of red wine
salt, and plenty of freshly ground black pepper

In a saucepan large enough to hold the meat comfortably, heat the fat and brown the meat all over. Remove the meat from the pan, set aside and brown the onions in the fat. Sprinkle with salt and pepper. Return the meat to the saucepan and surround with the pumpkin pieces and the prunes. Add the spices, one tablespoon of honey and the red wine. Cover the meat with cold water, cover the saucepan, and bring slowly to the boil. Simmer the pot gently for 3 hours. Taste the juices and add more honey if you think it needs it, and lots of black pepper. Serve very hot.

Passover Almond Cake

SERVES 10

Nuts played an important part in Passover food, often being used as a substitute for flour, as in this dessert. This could be served with one of the many Passover jams and preserves made in the weeks before the festival.

6 eggs
225 g / 8 oz light muscovado sugar
300 g / 10 oz ground almonds
juice of 1 lemon and the rind of 2 lemons

Heat the oven to 190 C / 375 F / Gas Mark 5. Separate the eggs and beat the egg yolks with the muscovado sugar until it is light and fluffy. Fold in the almonds, the lemon rind and the lemon juice. Whisk the egg white until they are stiff but not dry, and fold them into the almond mixture.

Thoroughly grease a 20 cm / 8 in cake tin or round baking ring. If you are concerned about it sticking, line the tin with greased greaseproof paper (baking parchment). Pour in the mixture and bake it for 40 minutes or until a skewer comes out clean. Turn the cake out onto a rack to cool. When cold, decorate or fill with fresh fruits.

9

An Imperial Birthday Banquet in the Forbidden City

The Emperor Qianlong was the fourth emperor of the Manchu (or Qing) dynasty, which ruled China from 1644 until the Republican Revolution in 1911. The majority of the Manchu emperors came to the throne as small children, but Qianlong was twenty-five when he inherited his empire, along with an authoritarian, centralized administration which was to oversee the territorial expansion of China to its widest limits during the course of his sixty-year reign. Qianlong was far from being a warrior emperor, however. A keen poet, writer and calligrapher, he produced three collections of essays and five albums of poetry, while encouraging literature, music and the applied arts at his court.

OPPOSITE The throne room of the Palace of Heavenly Purity in the Forbidden City.

Indeed it was his desire to have every kind of Chinese opera represented at his eightieth birthday in 1790 which led to the formation of the Beijing Opera as we know it. So impressed was he with the troupes from Anhui and Hubei Provinces that he insisted they remain to work with the Beijing troupe. Today the clown, child and female roles in the Beijing Opera sing in the Beijing dialect, while the male and more serious adult roles sing in the Hubei and Anhui dialects.

Qianlong was also a keen huntsman and traveller, making regular trips the length and breadth of his empire. Nonetheless 'home' remained the Forbidden City in Beijing, with its labyrinth of palaces and gardens.

LEFT *Inaugural Portrait of Emperor Qianlong* by Giuseppe Castiglione, 1736. Castiglione was an Italian missionary and amateur painter who settled in China in about 1715. A court favourite, he received many commissions from Qianlong.

Porcelain vase with 'famille rose' enamel decoration, peach branch and flowers, Qing dynasty.

The emperor normally ate two formal meals each day – breakfast at round 6am and a main meal between midday and 2pm, sometimes followed by a snack in the late afternoon. These meals would happen in whatever part of the Forbidden City the emperor chose to be for that meal. The actual meal was governed by a strict and complex etiquette.

What the emperor ate was as carefully monitored as how he ate it. Chinese philosophy, requiring all matter to be in a state of balance and 'harmony', was applied to food as much as to any other aspect of life. The emperor's diet therefore could not be monotonous or merely a simple mixture of ingredients, but had to be a harmonious blending of various elements. The emperor's meals had to include five cereals and foods with the five 'flavours' (sweet, bitter, sour, salty and spicy). Only thus could all the nutrients be obtained to stimulate the appetite and maintain good health. In addition, the emperor was served food and drink with specific health or medicinal properties – such as Zuangyuan wine to stimulate the spleen and the kidneys; Songling Taiping (longevity wine), a medicinal wine for older people; digestive aids such as watermelon juices, papaya and pineapple extract, peppermint tea, ginger cakes or the medicinal herbs rehmannia or ginko preserved in syrup. In Qianlong's case this careful approach certainly seems to have paid off, since he lived to the ripe old age of eighty-eight.

To ensure the diversity needed to create this 'harmony', raw materials came from all over China. From the north came ducks of every kind, fish, deer, bear, wild fowl, wild game and edible birds' nests; along with small root vegetables, bamboo shoots, lily, Chinese yam and mountain pears. From Shandong came peanuts, dates, persimmons and lotus seeds; from Henan came lilies and preserved peaches. Sweet-scented osmanthus blossoms and Hami melons came from Shaanxi; from Guangdong came oranges, lychees, tangerines and round cardamom; from Zhejang came crystal sugar, palms and longan (small lychees); more fresh fruits came from Hunan; and from northeastern China came plums, pears, hazel-nuts, hawthorn berries and grapes. Vegetables were grown locally and bought daily at the markets, but pickles and salted vegetables were sent as tributes from every part of the empire. To ensure that the emperor got the benefit of such diversity, every meal had to include a wide range of these ingredients, combining meats and vegetables, sweet and salty pastries, thin and thick soups, pickles, rice and wheat, all served as both hot and cold dishes. This led to a minimum of thirty dishes for an everyday meal, and for a banquet to mark as important an occasion as the emperor's birthday the number of dishes was well into the hundreds.

The emperor's eightieth birthday was the occasion of great celebrations lasting over many months, but the culmination was the Birthday Banquet served in the Palace of Heavenly Purity in the Forbidden City. In a country where regulations laid down the number of lychees you should have in your bowl according to your rank, such an occasion, with its hundreds of important guests, must have been an organizational nightmare for the Banqueting Office and the Imperial Household Department. Ranged according to rank and importance, guests were placed progressively further from the emperor. Their invitation was received only when they had pledged a gift of ingredients to the Banqueting Office. For example, a prince of the second degree was expected to provide eight tables, three sheep and three jars of liquor, while a prince of the third degree provided three tables, two sheep and two jars. The lower your rank, the fewer dishes you could expect to be served. Birthday banquets were ranked fourth in the Banqueting Office's hierarchy, and as such the regulations laid down precisely how much of each food was to appear:

> At each table there would be 4 dishes of flaky pastry square and pies, each dish holding 48 pieces and each piece weighing 55gm; 1 dish of flaky pastry with honey, holding 48 pieces and each pieces weighing 70gm; 2 dishes of small steamed buns, each holding 20 pieces and each piece weighing 45gm... 6 dishes of fresh fruits holding each 10 tangerines, mandarin oranges, apples, yellow pear and red pears...

and so the list continued on and on.

The main banquet table was placed in the centre of the Hall of Heavenly Purity, draped with 'a glittering yellow cover embroidered with golden dragons and sewn with semi precious stones'. This was laid with eight rows of offerings — a row of hot meat dishes and a row of cold meat dishes; one of hot vegetarian dishes and one of cold vegetarian dishes; rows of fresh fruit and 'titbits'; and rows of steamed food and vases of flowers. The emperor's personal table was set with

Lotus painting. Hanging scroll, Qing dynasty.

a spoon of zitan wood inlaid with gold filigree, ivory chopsticks inlaid with gold, a small gold basin and a gold spittoon. However, this was only the start. Once the emperor had tasted from his banqueting table, it was removed and was replaced by a 'feasting table' from which he was offered a further forty dishes – twenty of meat and twenty varieties of fruit. Throughout the banquet songs and dances were performed. The whole affair lasted for four hours, from the first laying of the tables at 11am until the emperor departed at 3pm.

Realistically, there is no way of reproducing anything seriously resembling the emperor's birthday banquet – unless you plan to be eating it for a month. I have therefore chosen a selection of what I hope will be harmoniously balanced dishes to represent the type of food that the emperor might have eaten, which will at least give you a flavour of the Qing banquet. Maybe you could imagine that you are only being offered a twentieth portion of the dishes on offer to the higher tables!

You will need to spend at least an hour in a Chinese supermarket before you start on your feast. You should be able to find one in the Chinese quarter of any reasonable size town but if not, ask a local Chinese restaurant if they could help with ingredients. Amongst the many amazing foods on the supermarket shelves you will find ready-made steamed buns, both plain and stuffed. Making steamed buns is an art in itself, so I would suggest that you buy them ready-made and just steam them according to the instructions on the pack and add them to the dishes on your festive table. You should allow one large and one small bun per person.

To be true to the emperor's table arrangements you need to lay all the dishes out on the table together so that your guests can pick from each as they fancy. However, you may wish to use the bean curd recipe as an appetiser. Since the main feasting table consisted of twenty dishes of meat and twenty of fruit, I suggest that you serve several large platters of fresh seasonal fruits for dessert.

Detail from bowl of 'famille rose' enamel, Qing dynasty. In Chinese tradition, butterflies symbolize longevity. They are often seen on items given as birthday gifts.

Although the records of the Banqueting Office are extremely detailed, they do not, sadly, include any recipes. I have therefore adapted a number of classic Chinese recipes which just might have been used to create the emperor's feast.

Marinated Bean Curd

SERVES 8–10

The bean curd should be classed as a 'titbit' and so could have appeared on the emperor's banqueting table. You can serve it as part of the main feast or as an appetizer before the meal.

400 g / 14 oz fresh bean curd/tofu
2 tablespoons light soya sauce
1 teaspoon sesame oil
2 scant teaspoons muscovado sugar
2 teaspoons very finely chopped fresh ginger root
6 finely chopped spring onions (scallions)
1 teaspoon chilli oil
sea salt and freshly ground pepper

Cut the bean curd into bite-size cubes and put into a small serving dish. Combine all the other ingredients thoroughly and use to dress the bean curd, tossing it gently. Chill for 2–24 hours before serving.

Spinach and Bean Curd Soup

SERVES 8–10

This and the duck hot pot on page 113 are intended to balance each other out as a light vegetarian soup and a rich, meat-based soup. Both are quite filling but totally delicious, albeit completely different in character.

8 dried Chinese mushrooms, soaked in hot water for 30 minutes
300 g / 10 oz young fresh spinach
400 g / 14 oz fresh bean curd cut into bite size cubes
2 tablespoons sunflower oil
100 g / 4 oz fresh field mushrooms, sliced thinly
2 tablespoons light soy sauce
2 tablespoons Shaoxing wine
1 litre / 1¾ pints / 4¼ cups good vegetable stock
4 level teaspoons cornflour (cornstarch), mixed with a little water
sea salt and freshly ground pepper to taste
2 teaspoons sesame oil

Three people eating and drinking, 17th century. Two female attendants in the foreground bring food and wine to the table.

Soak the mushrooms in boiling water for 30 minutes then drain, remove the stems and slice very finely. Blanch the spinach in boiling water for a minute, then rinse in cold water, drain, squeeze dry and chop finely. Blanch the beancurd in boiling water for 10 minutes, then drain and leave to dry.

Heat the sunflower oil in a wok over high heat. Add the dried and fresh mushrooms and cook for a minute, stirring. Add the spinach, soy sauce and wine, and stir for another minute. Add the stock, cornflour (cornstarch), water, bean curd, salt and pepper. Bring back to the boil and simmer for 4–5 minutes. Sprinkle with sesame oil and serve at once.

Boiled Pork with Minced Garlic

SERVES 8–10

This is a cold meat dish, to counterbalance the hot meat of the duck hot pot. Although the recipe is simple and sounds quite unappealing, the results are really excellent. The pork is mouth-wateringly tender and absorbs the flavours of the sauce beautifully. Cook it several hours in advance to give the meat time to absorb fully all the multiple tastes of the sauce.

1 kilo / 2¼ lb lean loin of pork, boned and rolled
8 spring onions (scallions) chopped
2 thick slices of ginger root, peeled
600 ml / 1 pint / 2½ cups water
4 tablespoons peanut oil
8 large cloves garlic, peeled and chopped very finely
2 level teaspoons each sea salt and muscovado sugar
2 tablespoons rice vinegar
2 tablespoons soy sauce
2 teaspoons chilli oil

Put the pork in a heavy pot with the spring onions (scallions), ginger and water. Bring to the boil and simmer, covered, for 45 minutes. Remove the pork and cool slightly. Keep the cooking water for stock; discard the ginger and spring onions.

Slice the pork thinly with the grain and lay out on a serving dish. Heat the peanut oil in a wok and stir-fry the garlic for a minute. Remove from the heat and mix in the sea salt, sugar, rice vinegar, soy sauce and chilli oil. Spoon over the pork slices and leave to marinate for a couple of hours. Serve at room temperature.

Hot Pot of Duck with Ginko Nuts

SERVES 8–10

1 large duck with giblets if possible
2 litres / 3½ pints / 8½ cups good stock
largish piece of root ginger (around 50 g /2 oz), peeled but left whole
6 pieces of dried citrus peel
1 heaped teaspoon sea salt
2 tablespoons ginkgo nuts
1 medium size Chinese cabbage, sliced thinly
2 tablespoons light soy sauce
4 tablespoons Shaoxing wine
2 spring onions (scallions), chopped

Remove the giblets and chop and reserve the liver. Cut the parson's nose and the surrounding fat away from the duck and place it in a heavy lidded casserole with the stock. Bring to the boil and simmer for 15 minutes, skimming any scum that rises to the top. Turn the duck off, allow to cool slightly, and remove any excess fat from the top of the pot.

Add the piece of ginger, the dried citrus peel and the salt. Bring back to the boil, cover and simmer gently for an hour, turning the duck every now and then.

Add the ginkgo nuts and continue to simmer for a further 30 minutes. Remove the duck from the soup and allow the latter to cool slightly. Remove any extra fat and the skin from the duck, and cut the flesh into thin strips. Skim off any extra fat which has risen to the surface of the soup.

Add the cabbage, soy sauce, wine, spring onions, chopped liver and sliced duck to the soup. Bring back to the boil and serve.

Jade dish, Qing dynasty. Many vessels were made of jade in the 18th century, as new sources of jade became available.

Stir-fried Salad with Pancake Strips

SERVES 8–10

Unusually for a salad, this improves with keeping and is better well-chilled than at room temperature, so aim to make it several hours before you plan to eat it.

10 large dried Chinese mushrooms
340 g / 12 oz cucumber, halved lengthwise and de-seeded
340 g / 12 oz carrots
1 large red pepper, de-seeded
15 spring onions (scallions)
8 tablespoons corn or sunflower oil
350 g / 12 oz beansprouts
4 tablespoons sesame paste

4 teaspoons water
4 tablespoons rice vinegar
1 scant teaspoon salt
10 turns of the peppermill
2 small eggs, lightly beaten

Soak the mushrooms for 30 minutes in boiling water, then squeeze out thoroughly and slice very thinly. Cut the cucumber into very thin slices, put in a dish, and sprinkle liberally with salt to draw out the extra water. Leave for 30 minutes then drain thoroughly. Cut the carrots into very thin slices, put into the dish and sprinkle liberally with salt to draw out the moisture. Leave for 30 minutes then drain thoroughly. Slice the red pepper very thinly. Halve the spring onions (scallions) lengthways, chop into 2 cm / 1 in pieces, and separate the green from the white.

Mix the sesame paste with half the water, stirring in the same direction. The mixture will thicken. Add the rest of the water, continue to stir and the mixture will thin. Gradually add the vinegar and seasoning.

Heat a wok over a high heat, then add 6 tablespoons of the oil and swirl around. Add the white spring onions and stir a couple of times. Add the mushrooms and then the red pepper and cook for a couple minutes, stirring all the time. Add the carrots and bean sprouts and cook vigorously, turning thoroughly, for about 2 minutes until the vegetables are just partially cooked and still crunchy. Add the spring onion greens, stir a couple more times, and turn onto a serving dish. Drain off any liquid which may ooze out.

Heat a large frying pan over a moderate heat. Add the remaining oil, making sure that the whole surface of the pan is covered. When the oil is hot, pour in the lightly beaten egg, tipping the pan to make sure that it reaches the very edge. When cooked on one side, loosen the edges of the pancake, flip it over, and cook until it is firm but not hard. Remove to a plate and, when it has cooled, cut into strips.

When the vegetables are cool mix in the cucumber. Stir the dressing and mix it well into the salad. Arrange the pancake strips in a lattice pattern on top. Cover and chill the salad before serving.

10

Georgian Christmas with Parson Woodforde

James Woodforde was not a particularly remarkable man. Born in 1740, he was the son of the vicar of Castle Cary in Somerset. He became a scholar at New College, Oxford, and was presented with the curacy of his father's parish at Castle Cary and the sub-wardenship of New College. He then became vicar of Weston Longueville, a village in Norfolk, when he was thirty-six. He never married, but in 1779 his niece Nancy came to stay with him and remained until his death in Weston in 1804.

What makes Parson Woodforde interesting to historians, and especially food historians, is that from the time that he first went up to Oxford in 1758 until his death he kept a detailed diary – in which he noted what he ate every day for dinner, and often for supper too. In Weston, Parson Woodforde mixed with the gentry of the county, dining with and entertaining local dignitaries on a regular basis. He employed at least four servants of his own and his house was often filled with visitors and their servants.

Although the Christmas holiday was celebrated, Christmas Day itself for the parson's family appears to have been much like any other day. On Christmas Eve in 1788, for example, he had the 'parlour Windows dressed as usual with Hulver-boughs well seeded with red berries, and likewise the kitchen'. But on Christmas Day, while Parson Woodforde read prayers and administered the Holy Sacrament, Nancy 'and Betsy Davy went off in the Norwich Chaise

LEFT Parson James Woodforde.

OPPOSITE *Buy my Goose, my fat Goose* by H. Merke. A tradesman has knocked on the door but his potential customers look unimpressed. Plate II of *Cries of London*, 1799.

[coach] ... to meet Mr Walker at the King's Head in Norwich, and there they dined, but returned home to Tea in the afternoon, Mr Walker with them'. The parson himself remained at home to provide the traditional Christmas dinner, which changed scarcely at all over the twenty-seven years of his residence, for the old men of the parish:

> Js Smith, Richard Buck, Thos. Cushing, Thos Carr, Richard Bates, Thos. Dicker and Thos Cary all dined at my House as is usual on Christmas Day. I gave each of them a Shilling to carry home to their Wives before they went away – in all 7s.od. I gave them for Dinner a piece of rost Beef and plumb Puddings – and after dinner half a Pint of strong Beer apiece.

Although Christmas Day at Weston may have been quite low key, that does not mean that it was ignored elsewhere. In 1773, when Woodforde was sub-warden at Oxford, he had the following Christmas dinner: 'two fine Codds boiled with fryed Souls around them and an oyster sauce, a fine Sirloin of Beef roasted, some peas soup and an orange pudding for first course. For the second we had a lease of Wild ducks, roasted, a fore quarter of lamb and sallad and mince pyes... After the second course there was a fine plumb cake'. These courses were interspersed with innumerable 'Grace Cups'. 'We dined at 3 o'clock', Woodforde noted, 'and were an Hour and a ½ at it. We all then went into the Senior Common Room where the Warden came and sat with us till prayers... We had rabbits roasted for supper as is usual on this day.'

In Weston, Christmas and New Year was a time for visiting. In 1778, just before Nancy came to live with him, the parson had ten people, including two children, visiting on the 23 December: 'all but Mr du Quesne spending the whole night with me being very dark and some falling rain'. A merry evening was obviously had by all as 'Mr Bodham, myself and Mr Donne sat up the whole night and played cards till 6 in the morning' while the rest of the guests disposed themselves around the house. The parson continues: 'around 6 in the morning we [Messers Bodham, Donne and Woodforde] serenaded the folks that were a bed with our best on the Hautboy [a type of oboe]'. The general merriment had obviously been helped along by the dinner that the parson had laid on: 'I gave them 3 fowls boiled, part of a Ham, the major part of which Ham was entirely eaten out by the Flies getting into

Illustration of holly from a French book on the forest trees of North America (1810-13).

it, a tongue boiled, a Leg of Mutton roasted, and an excellent currant pudding. I gave them for supper a couple of rabbit smothered in onions, some Hash Mutton and some Roasted potatoes.'

In 1790 the celebrations spilled over into New Year:

> Jan 1st. My brother and Wife, Mrs Clarke and Nancy breakfasted, dined and etc. here again. Mr and Mrs Custance and Mr du Quesne dined and spent the Afternoon with us, stayed until 8 and would have stayed longer but that their eldest Daughter was very bad with Scarlet Fever. We had for dinner today some Skaite and Oyster sauce, Peas Soup, Ham and Chicken, a boiled leg of Mutton with Capers, a rost Turkey, fried Rabbit, Brawn, Tarts, Mince pies and etc. Put into Mr Custance's coach as they returned home a quarter of the milk cheese that Mr Pounsett sent us. Mr Custance liked it very much at dinner. We had two tables at Cards this Evening, Whist and Quadrille. It was after 1 o'clock before I got to bed, my Brother being rather merry and very talkative.

The food that Parson Woodforde fed his neighbours and vistors was ample but simple: 'roast beef, roast turkey, boiled mutton, fryed rabbit, plum puddings, mince pies'. Nonetheless it is quite possible that a copy of Mrs Elizabeth Raffald's *Experienced English Housekeeper* could have been found in the kitchen or amongst Nancy' books. Elizabeth Raffald had been housekeeper at the estate of Sir Peter and Lady Warburton where she both learned her trade and met her husband, John Raffald, who was head gardener at the estate. After their marriage they left the Warburtons and opened a confectionery shop in Manchester which also sold ready-made dishes and elaborate centrepieces for the dining table. As the business prospered she included perfumes and cosmetics among her wares. She also started a registry (domestic agency), and managed to find time to have six daughters.

A Voluptuary under the horrors of Digestion by James Gillray, 1792. Satirical print of the Prince of Wales (later Prince Regent and George IV). He has demolished a heavy meal and a great deal of wine.

Mrs Elizabeth
Raffald, author of
*The Experienced English
Housekeeper*, first
published in 1768.

The Experienced English Housekeeper was published in 1768. In it Nancy would have
found everything she needed to run her uncle's household — plus a treasure trove
of delicious recipes. Most of the recipes for our Christmas dinner come from
here, with just one from Mrs Raffald's fellow cookery writer, Mrs Hannah Glasse.

Rolled Salmon
(Mrs Raffald)

SERVES 8

This dish is actually quite simple to make. Like so many 18th-century recipes it
tastes wonderfully fresh — especially if you use freshly grated nutmeg. Serve with
the dressed spinach dish on page 122.

1 medium (2 kilo / 4½ lb) salmon, boned and skinned but with the
two sides still in 1 piece
200 g / 7 oz mussels or clams, freshly cooked, frozen or tinned
1 large slice wholemeal (wholewheat) bread, crumbed
6 large sprigs of parsley, chopped
sea salt and freshly ground black pepper
½ freshly grated nutmeg
½ teaspoon ground mace
1 small head fennel, chopped
1 large bunch parsley
2 lemons
40 g / 1½ oz butter
40 g / 1½ oz flour
4 teaspoons grated horseradish (not horseradish cream or sauce)
90 ml / 3 fl oz / ⅜ cup medium sherry

Lay the 2 sides of salmon out on the counter, insides facing upwards, and arrange
the mussels, breadcrumbs and parsley down the middle of each. Generously
season them with salt and pepper, nutmeg and mace. Roll both up carefully and

The Fish Stall by William Kidd, *c.* 1830. The stallholder is cutting a codfish. A luscious-looking piece of salmon is on the table, along with other types of fish and seafood.

wrap or tie them in a piece of muslin to prevent them falling apart. If you do not have any muslin a new J cloth does very well.

Put both rolls in a pan just big enough to hold them with the fennel, parsley and one lemon, sliced, and cover with water. Cover the pan and bring it very slowly to the boil. Simmer for 5 minutes then turn off the heat. Leave the fish to continue cooking in the water for at least another hour. Remove the rolls of fish carefully from the pan and keep them warm. Strain the fish stock and reserve.

In a separate pan melt the butter gently. Add the flour, stir around well, then add the horseradish. Slowly, stirring all the time, add 400 ml (14 fl oz / 1¾ cups) of the fish stock. Continue to cook until the sauce thickens, then add the sherry and season to taste if it needs it.

Remove the muslin from the 2 salmon rolls and place them in the middle of a serving dish. Surround with the dressed spinach and decorate with the remaining lemon, sliced and formed into butterflies. Serve the sauce separately.

Dressed Spinach
(Mrs Raffald)

SERVES 8

This is a really simple dish but, as Mrs Raffald says, 'it will eat exceeding mild, and quite a different taste from the common way'. Despite the large quantity of butter, it does not taste overly rich.

1.5 kg / 3½ lb fresh spinach, well washed
200 g / 7 oz good quality butter
½ freshly grated nutmeg

Bring about 5 cm / 2 in of water to the boil in a large pan. Put in all the spinach and cook it briskly for a couple of minutes, turning all the time, until it is well wilted. Turn into a colander and press out as much water as possible.

In a clean pan, melt the butter. Add the spinach and mix well into the butter. Cook gently over a low heat, stirring from time to time, for 30–40 minutes or until all the water in the spinach has evaporated and it has absorbed most of the butter.

Just before serving, grate the nutmeg over the spinach. Serve with Mrs Raffald's salmon roll or any other meat or fish dish.

Ducks a la Mode
(Hannah Glasse)

SERVES 8

The wild ducks mentioned by Parson Woodforde might be a bit tough for this recipe from Hannah Glasse's *Art of Cookerie Made Plain and Easy*, but it is delicious with 21st-century domesticated ducks.

Creamware plate decorated with a scene from Aesop's *Fables* (The Cock and the Fox), 1770–75.

2 medium ducks with giblets

75 g / 3 oz butter

1 tablespoon olive oil

2 medium onions, peeled and chopped roughly

1 medium carrot, scrubbed and diced

2 rashers of streaky bacon, chopped

4 mushrooms, chopped

1 heaped tablespoon flour

large glass of red wine

900 ml / 1½ pints / 3¾ cups water or stock

2 sprigs parsley

2 bouquet garni

freshly ground black pepper

2 tablespoons seasoned flour

4 anchovy fillets, chopped very small.

4 shallots or small onions, peeled and chopped very small

300 ml / ½ pint / 1¼ cups Marsala or sweet red wine

a large bunch of fresh herbs — parsley, thyme, bayleaves

2 lemons

Take two fine ducks, cut them into Quarters, fry them in Butter a little Brown, then pour out all the Fat, and throw a little Flour over them; add Half a Pint of good Gravy, a Quarter of a Pint of Red wine, two Shalots, an Anchovy, and a Bundle of Sweet Herbs; cover them close and let them stew a Quarter of an Hour; take out the Herbs, skim off the Fat, and let your Sauce be as thick as Cream. Send to the Table and garnish with Lemon.

Remove the giblets from the ducks. Set the liver aside. Heat 25 g of butter and 1 oz of the oil in a heavy pan and add the onions, carrot, bacon and mushrooms. Fry briskly for 5 –10 minutes, stirring frequently to prevent it burning, or until the vegetables are well tanned. Add the flour and continue to cook and stir for a further few minutes until the flour is also lightly browned.

Gradually add the wine, stirring continually, and then the stock or water. Add the giblets, parsley and bouquet garni. Bring to boil, reduce to a simmer, and cook at a gentle simmer for an hour. Strain the gravy and season with black pepper and lightly with sea salt if it needs it.

Joint the duck into 4 breasts and 4 legs, removing any excess fat or skin. You can use the carcass and wings to make an excellent duck soup.

Heat the remaining butter in 1 large or 2 smaller heavy lidded pans. Briskly fry the duck joints until they are lightly browned on all sides. Remove onto kitchen paper (towel) and pat dry. Throw out the excess fat or reserve for other purposes. Wipe the inside of the pan or pans with kitchen paper (towel). Roll the joints well in the seasoned flour and return them to the pans.

Chop the duck liver very small and add to the pans, along with the chopped anchovy and onions. Add 600 ml / 1 pint / 2½ cups of the gravy and the Marsala along with the herbs, well tied together. Ensure that the liver, onion, anchovy and herbs are well submerged in the sauce.

Bring to the boil, cover and reduce to a simmer for 30 minutes. Remove the herbs and adjust the seasoning to taste. Grate the rind from the lemons and add to the sauce. Squeeze the juice and add gradually to your own taste.

Serve the duck joints with the sauce spooned over the top. Serve with the dressed spinach or another green vegetable of your choice, lightly steamed.

A Mince Pye

SERVES 8

The plumb puddings that the Parson served to his 'old men' every year would have been solid steamed puddings, rather too heavy after our Christmas dinner. But even the mince pies which appeared on his table would have been more substantial than a modern mince pie.

In the 18th century the 'mincemeat' with which the pie was filled was just that

— minced meat to which was added substantial quantities of dried fruits and spices to help keep it fresh. In the days before refrigeration and speedy transport, keeping meat and fish fresh until it could be eaten was a serious problem. The acidity of the fruit and the preservative quality of the spices did much to 'extend shelf life'. In Mrs Raffald's recipe the balance of the ingredients is already tipping towards the fruits, so you will find that you can scarcely taste the meat.

350 g / 12 oz wholemeal flour
200 g / 7 oz butter or butter and lard mixed
water to mix
50 g / 2 oz shredded beef suet
100 g / 4 oz currants
100 g / 4 oz raisins
50 g / 2 oz dark muscovado sugar
285 g / 10 oz apple, peeled, cored and grated coarsely
200 g / 7 oz cold tongue, or 'salt boiled beef', chopped small
1 level teaspoon each grated nutmeg and ground cinnamon
½ teaspoon each of ground cloves and ground mace
50 g / 2 oz candied orange or lemon peel
100 ml / 3 fl oz / ⅜ cup brandy
1 egg

Rub the fat into the flour and mix to a stiff paste with cold water. Roll out and line a 25 cm / 10 in flan dish, leaving enough pastry for the lid. Mix all the filling ingredients thoroughly together, then fill the flan dish.

Cover with a lid, pierce it to let the steam out, and decorate with pastry balls or holly leaves. Beat the egg and paint the top of the pie to make it shine. Bake the pie in a moderate oven (180 C / 350 F / Gas Mark 4) for 30–40 minutes or until the pastry is browned and firm. Remove from the oven and allow to cool. Serve warm or cold.

Mrs Raffald would probably not have served the pies with cream or custard as there would have been other desserts on the table which would have filled that role. However, you may prefer to serve the pie with cream or ice cream.

Pistachio Cream

SERVES 8

Although they do not seem to have appeared very often at Weston, 'creams' were great favourites with 18th-century cooks. *The Experienced English Housekeeper* contains no less than 17 'cream' recipes, including Spanish Cream, Ribband Cream, Steeple Cream with Wine sour, Raspberry Cream, Tea Cream and La Pompadour Cream. The Pistachio Cream not only tastes delicious but looks very pretty. However, it will turn into scrambled eggs if it boils as you make it.

80 g / 3 oz shelled pistachio nuts
2 tablespoons brandy
3 medium egg yolks
600 ml / 1 pint / 2½ cups double (heavy) cream
1 tablespoon Cointreau or Orange Curacao

Reserving a few for decoration, grind the pistachio nuts in a food processor with the brandy. Avoid over-grinding them into a paste. In a saucepan, mix the egg yolks with the cream. Add the nuts and cook very gently, stirring continually, until the cream thickens. Do not allow the mixture to boil. When it has thickened slightly, add the liqueur and pour into 8 tall glasses – champagne glasses are ideal.

Allow to cool or chill. When cold, decorate with the remaining pistachio nuts. Serve with ratafia biscuits.

Further Reading

THE RETURN OF ODYSSEUS: A HOMERIC BANQUET

Andrew Dalby, *Siren Feasts: A History of Food and Gastronomy in Greece* (Routledge)
Andrew Dalby and Sally Grainger, *The Classical Cookbook* (British Museum Press)

DINING AT THE COURT OF LUCREZIA BORGIA

Anna del Conte has written over a dozen books on Italian food, all of which are a delight both to read and to cook from. However, if you are interested in the historical aspects, her *Gastronomy of Italy* (Pavilion) gives most historical information.

HIAWATHA'S WEDDING FEAST

Beverly Cox and Martin Jacobs, *Spirit of the Harvest: North American Indian Cooking* (Stewart, Tabori & Chang)

BANQUETING WITH MUGHAL EMPERORS

Joyce Westrip, *Moghal Cooking: India's Courtly Cuisine* (Serif)
Bamber Gascoigne, *The Great Moghals: India's Most Flamboyant Rulers* (Robinson)
Julie Sahni, *Classic Indian Cooking* (Dorling Kindersley)

THE CUISINE OF THE AZTECS

Sophie Coe, *America's First Cuisines* (University of Texas Press)
Sophie and Michael Coe, *The True History of Chocolate* (Thames & Hudson)
Sara Jayne Stanes, *Chocolate: The Definitive Guide* (Grub Street)

JEWISH PASSOVER SUPPER: CENTURIES OF TRADITION

Claudia Roden, *The Book of Jewish Food: An Odyssey from Samarkand to Vilna and the Present Day* (Viking)
Oded Schwarz, *In Search of Plenty: A History of Jewish Food* (Kyle Cathie)

AN IMPERIAL BIRTHDAY BANQUET IN THE FORBIDDEN CITY

Vivienne and Jenny Lo, *150 Recipes from the Teahouse* (Faber & Faber)
Yan Kit So, *Classic Chinese Cookbook* (Dorling Kindersley)

Index